Furnishing Williamsburg's Historic Buildings

Furnishing Williamsburg's Historic Buildings

By
Jan Kirsten Gilliam
and
Betty Crowe Leviner

The Colonial Williamsburg Foundation
Williamsburg, Virginia

WILLIAMSBURG DECORATIVE ARTS SERIES
Graham Hood, *Editor*

Chelsea Porcelain at Williamsburg
    by John C. Austin

English and Oriental Carpets at Williamsburg
    by Mildred B. Lanier

English Silver at Williamsburg
    by John D. Davis

Furnishing Williamsburg's Historic Buildings
    by Jan Kirsten Gilliam and Betty Crowe Leviner

The Governor's Palace in Williamsburg: A Cultural Study
    by Graham Hood

New England Furniture at Williamsburg
    by Barry A. Greenlaw

*Rebellion and Reconciliation: Satirical Prints on
    the Revolution at Williamsburg*
    by Joan D. Dolmetsch

The Williamsburg Collection of Antique Furnishings

Wallace Gallery Decorative Arts Publications

Eighteenth-Century Clothing at Williamsburg
    by Linda Baumgarten

Worcester Porcelain in the Colonial Williamsburg Collection
    by Samuel M. Clarke

Library of Congress Cataloging-in-Publication Data

Gilliam, Jan (Jan Kirsten)
    Furnishing Williamsburg's historic buildings.
        p.   cm.—(Williamsburg decorative arts series)
    Prepared by Jan Gilliam and Betty Leviner.
    Includes bibliographical references and index.
    ISBN 0-87935-083-0
    1. Furniture—Virginia—Williamsburg—History—18th century.
    2. House furnishings—Virginia—Williamsburg—History—18th-century.
    I. Leviner, Betty (Betty Crowe)   II. Title.   III. Series.
    NK2438.W54G5   1991
    747.2155'4252'09033—dc20

Book design: Vernon Wooten.

Printed and bound in Hong Kong

Frontispiece: *Conversation Group:
Family gathered around table with
architectural model.* Artist unknown. Oil
on canvas. England, third quarter of the
eighteenth century. G 1957–196.

Contents

Illustrations

Foreword

Many people feel that the past is all they can rely on in a world that changes frighteningly fast. Yet the past changes too, continually, for historians and others who take the time to look at it intently. Much of the change is admittedly in protean detail or subtle shifts of shading while the great landmarks remain firm and clear, but even differences in shading and highlighting can produce new pictures, new images of the ways that people of the past lived and worked, how they arranged their houses no less than how they arranged their lives.

The idea of re-creating eighteenth-century interiors with authentic fabrics and household furnishings as little arenas where life was lived and where the past becomes real and immediate and alive is still provocative after a hundred years or more of experiment. Curators at Colonial Williamsburg have been doing it on an expansive scale since 1930 and the challenge to get ever closer to the authentic past is still exciting. For some people the past comes alive most dramatically or poignantly through written documents, or archaeology, or the fabric of buildings. For curators it is objects that embody the special quality of the living past, and for skilled, dedicated young curators like Betty Leviner and Jan Gilliam it is the way that the objects relate to each other in defined architectural spaces that produces the special thrill of touching history and "being there."

Paintings and prints, which provide us with much of the evidence for how the past actually *looked*, are small windows into a past that is still living. Through them we see earlier places, people, and times, characters who are convincing in their sense of physical presence, their gestures apposite, the clutter of their living authentic. Thus we study paintings and prints of the period to help us re-create on a human scale the interiors and environments that can so convincingly impart a sense of the physically immediate past.

This book has been a labor of love for Betty Leviner and her assistant, Jan Gilliam, and we are grateful that they have made the fruits of their own work in recent years—and that of their predecessors at Colonial Williamsburg—so accessible.

Graham Hood

"To my husband, John Hyman, who made even burdensome days light."—Betty

"To my parents for their love and encouragement, and to Kevin, Bruce, and Kari for their persistent interest."—Jan

Preface

This book had its beginnings several years ago as more and more visitors to Colonial Williamsburg commented on changes that were taking place in the exhibition buildings in the Historic Area. Window curtains were disappearing right and left, oriental carpets were being taken up, and furniture was being pushed back against the walls. While historical interpreters did their best to explain these changes to our visitors, the curatorial division saw an opportunity to document and elucidate the rationale behind the transformation. The result is this book. In it we have illustrated our reasoning for implementing a wide variety of alterations that have occurred in Colonial Williamsburg's exhibition buildings over past decades. We wanted to demonstrate that these changes were not capricious or whimsical but were based on professional research and analysis of both documentary and graphic sources.

We hope our book will be of use both to the interested layperson and to other museum professionals. At the end we have included a glossary to explain terms in their eighteenth-century context. The bibliography contains sources used in writing this book as well as other publications that provide further information on a variety of related topics. While the text has been fully endnoted, we have chosen to exclude notes from the captions since the information can easily be found in the bibliography.

In producing this volume, we have been grateful for the help and advice of many of our colleagues. We would like to thank all of our co-workers in the Department of Collections, especially Jay Gaynor, Liza Gusler, Hans Lorenz, Craig McDougal, and Laurie Suber. Our special thanks to Graham Hood who initiated this project and keep our spirits up throughout its duration. We also appreciate the comments of those who read the various drafts—Robert Birney, Cathleene Hellier, Dennis O'Toole, Linda Rowe, and Beatrix Rumford. We are especially grateful to Mark R. Wenger for reading over the final draft and giving freely of his time and expertise and to Willie Graham for providing two architectural drawings. Our thanks to the managers and supervisors who went out of their way to help us coordinate the photography, particularly John Hamant, formerly manager of special events for the Company of Colonial Performers. Thanks, too, to Kevin Burke who brought our ideas and illustrations to life with his sensitive photography, as did all the Colonial Williamsburg staff who appeared in costume. This book could not have been completed without the support, advice, and patience of Donna Sheppard, Joseph Rountree, and Vernon Wooten in the Publications Department.

Finally, we would like our families to know how much we each appreciate their continued support during this project.

Fig. 1

Governor's Palace Dining Room Post-1981. The inventory listed not only
furnishings associated with dining, but also desks (not shown) and tables to assist
in conducting business. The refurnished room now reflects the multipurpose use
of the space, which was a common feature of many eighteenth-century rooms.

Introduction

Over the past decades, the curators at Colonial Williamsburg have been involved in an ongoing process of reexamining period objects as well as the period context in which these objects were used. As a result of this continuing investigation into eighteenth-century Williamsburg and eastern Virginia, we came to realize that the furnishings in many of our exhibition buildings did not accurately reflect the way in which various objects were used or displayed in the dwellings of two hundred years ago. Additional and ongoing research has resulted in modifications—extensive in some instances, relatively modest in others. The winds of change began to be felt in the 1970s when a new look was taken at the Raleigh Tavern that resulted in furnishing changes. After that came the reinstallation of the butler's pantry at the Governor's Palace. However, the most dramatic example of these changes in approach and perception was the refurnishing of nearly every exhibition space in the Palace in 1981. Based primarily on the inventory taken in October 1770 after the death of Lord Botetourt, the Palace refurnishing was a time-consuming project that culminated in the changes a visitor now sees (figs. 1 and 2). Other exhibition buildings in Colonial Williamsburg's Historic Area have subsequently experienced modifications in their furnishings. These changes were made gradually as new insights into the past suggested more authentic ways to interpret the exhibition buildings. If the interiors at Williamsburg now are compared with those of a decade ago, it is clear that

Fig. 2

Governor's Palace Dining Room Pre-1981. This photograph was taken prior to the 1981 refurnishing. Before that date, the room was interpreted as the formal dining room. A bowfat in which glass and other tablewares were stored was specified in the inventory, but it was missing from the space before the 1981 refurnishing. It now appears in the refurnished room.

Fig. 3

Gaol "Dining Room." Prior to its refurnishing, the gaol contained two rooms, the living room and dining room, both modern terms for these spaces. Since the gaol was not only a place for criminals and debtors but also the living quarters for the gaoler and his family, this portion of the building should be devoted to the family's quarters.

the transformations which have taken place in other exhibition buildings are no less remarkable than those at the Palace (figs. 3 and 4).

Why do the buildings look different today? Were the curators of the past not interested in authenticity? Were they wrong? The evolution of the furnishings in the buildings does not reflect a prior lack of research so much as it does ever-new insights, subtle changes in philosophy, and new perceptions of the colonial period in American history. The scholarship of the 1980s and 1990s is not the same as that of the 1930s or the 1960s, the time when many of the exhibition buildings were originally furnished. It is now less important than it once was to give priority in room displays to aesthetically superior objects. Historians and curators are continually exploring new aspects of eighteenth-century objects and history. Consideration of the social uses of the objects and the spaces in which they were placed differs from the previous perceptions of objects as primarily decorative pieces. New insights into the kinds of furnishings made and used in Williamsburg have caused us to look again at the items located in many of

the rooms. Thus changing perspectives, as well as the discovery of hitherto
unknown documentary sources and the reexamination of long-known
evidence, result in the refinement of room interiors so that they may more
accurately reflect the life-styles of the past.

   Some of the most useful sources to aid in the furnishing of interior
rooms are the prints and paintings created in the eighteenth century.
Some graphics portray eighteenth-century interiors as seen through the
eyes of contemporaries. The paintings depicting groupings, usually
families, known as conversation pieces were not done as formal portraits
but instead captured the family in a relaxed, informal moment at home
rather than in a studio. While the family or artist might have chosen to
embellish the setting somewhat, the furnishings nonetheless reveal much
about eighteenth-century taste and decorating habits. Informal family
portraits, along with satirical and illustrative prints, provide a way of
seeing how these spaces functioned and how they might have appeared

Fig. 4

*Gaol Bedchamber. After researching many aspects of gaolers and other middle-
class families, it became evident that the presence of a room devoted to dining
was inappropriate for a middling household. Rather, the living space for a family
should consist of a first-floor bedchamber as well as the all-purpose hall. The
family could have eaten in either space, but for more privacy they could enjoy
their meals in the bedchamber.*

when in use. Since graphics portraying colonial Virginia interiors are
rare, it is possible to study English sources because of the close ties many
wealthy Virginians had with the Mother Country and the similarities
resulting from this connection (fig. 5).

Many visitors today, when viewing the exhibition spaces, com-
ment on how bare the rooms look. This reaction is due partly to the fact
that they have grown accustomed to the eighteenth century as it was
modified by the nineteenth century. Although furnished with eighteenth-century antiques, many room displays in museums were arranged
in a nineteenth-century manner, which meant filling the rooms with
objects that originally might not have been used in that context. The
Victorians' love of knickknacks, photos, plants, and fabrics as decorating items contrasted starkly with the "neat and plain" style favored by
Virginians in the eighteenth century (fig. 6). What the Victorians
perceived as an authentic "colonial look" is now referred to as Colonial
Revival—the nineteenth-century American idea of the way in which
colonists arranged their homes.

Many times this perception of the rooms as empty stems from
viewing the room "at rest." When a room was not in use in the eighteenth century, the tables and chairs were generally placed neatly

against the walls (fig. 7). This placement made it easier to arrange furniture in the center of the room to accommodate several activities depending on the time of day and needs of the host. Despite being described as a dining room or parlor, these rooms were not used exclusively for one purpose. If the furnishings of a room in an exhibition building are compared to those of a room in a period painting or inventory, the amount of furniture in each is very similar; yet because the room that appears in the painting portrays people and activity, it looks more crowded (fig. 8). As they are now furnished, some exhibition spaces are set up to reflect the activities of the household, while others

Fig. 6

George Wythe House Parlor before Changes. This room has several colonial revival features. The spinning wheel, while a popular icon of the colonial era, was not present in the parlor, which was a space for entertaining, but rather belonged in a work setting. The window curtains and sofa are eighteenth-century features as well, but were not common in most Virginia parlors of the period.

Fig. 7

*Brush-Everard House Dining
Room. The chairs are lined up
against the wall along with the
dining table like those in figure 5.
The center of the room is empty
since the present activity in the
house is shown as having taken
place in the parlor across the
passage. The six prints that composed Hogarth's Marriage-a-la-
Mode series hang on the walls. In
the period, Colonel Thomas Jones
of Virginia owned several Hogarth
prints including this series.*

are left "at rest." If we can imagine these spaces with ladies in full, colorful
gowns and gentlemen in breeches and embroidered waistcoats, the rooms
take on a livelier atmosphere.

Visual sources are not the sole basis of information when furnishing
the interiors; graphics must be used in conjunction with written documents, architectural evidence, and archaeological analysis in order to
complete the picture. While English graphic sources have frequently been
relied on in this book, they have been used together with Virginia inventories, diaries, letters, and extant buildings to create accurate eighteenth-
century colonial interiors. Many eighteenth-century household furnishings such as ceramics, metals, furniture, and so forth exist today, and thus
were used in various groupings within the houses. Inventories can sometimes indicate how many pieces of each type of object were in a room and
in which particular room they were kept. Each inventory documents the
type of goods one individual had accumulated for his house. When
several of these are studied as a group, for instance by location or estate
value, they reveal furnishing and consumer trends that help us to plan the
interiors of houses that are typical for the area. The York County project,
a study of inventories specifically for this area, has aided us in our en-
deavor to be regionally accurate. Architectural evidence gives an idea of

Fig. 8

The Story of Pamela, Plate X. Line engraving. England, 1744. This print depicts a scene from the popular eighteenth-century novel Pamela. Because of the presence of the ladies, it is not immediately evident that the portion of the room shown is furnished with only a couple of chairs and a table. Once the ladies leave the room, only the table and chairs on the carpet will be left as a reminder of their presence. 1968-280, 10.

the size of the space in which all these pieces had to fit as well at that space's architectural embellishment (fig. 9). Archaeological finds can reveal what types of items (particularly ceramics) were used on the site. Once all items from a particular site have been retrieved from the ground and carefully documented and analyzed, a more complete story emerges that can potentially tell us what kinds of foods were eaten, how they were prepared, what tablewares were used by which individuals,

Fig. 9

George Wythe House Dining Room. Since the Wythe House is an original building, the room's window placement and size are the same as they were in the eighteenth century and suggest how furniture might have fit in the allotted space. Between the windows is the only place large enough to accommodate a side table (not shown). Evidence that a bowfat was originally in the corner determines the placement of the ceramics in this room.

Fig. 10

A Group Portrait, Probably of the Raikes Family by Gawen Hamilton. Oil on canvas. England, 1730-1732. This family is gathered around the table possibly enjoying dessert with fruit and drinks. The table and chairs have been set in the center of the room for this event. The servants on the left are serving drinks from the sideboard table and cleaning the glasses in the cistern below the marble table. Courtesy, Yale Center for British Art, Paul Mellon Collection.

and more. It is the graphic sources, though, that reveal the typical ways of arranging pieces within the given structure, and, to some extent, how those pieces were used and enjoyed by the owners. The various elements needed for a room survive as separate entities; it is the print or painting that ultimately depicts how to put it all together in an eighteenth-century setting (fig. 10).

Reliance on paintings, prints, and other extant sources provides information dealing mainly with the upper classes of society. The artists of the period naturally painted people who could afford the cost of luxuries. Surviving documents and objects also come chiefly from wealthier individuals because they descended in the family or were preserved because of their beauty and quality. The lack of detailed information about the middling and lower classes makes it more difficult to reconstruct their daily lives and material world. The exhibition houses in Williamsburg primarily feature the living spaces of the middling and upper strata of Virginia society and give the visitor a detailed look at the life-style of the town's gentry in the second half of the eighteenth century. While it is more difficult to portray domestic settings for the other townspeople accurately, an idea of their lives can be garnered from such exhibition areas as the outbuildings, trade shops, and the three exhibition buildings that housed middling families.

The following chapters form a detailed study, by room, of the houses of the wealthier townspeople in Virginia's colonial capital. By looking at each room separately, it is possible to pay close attention to what is appropriate for the space and why. Because the interpretation at Colonial Williamsburg focuses around the year 1770, many of the furnishing decisions are made on the basis of information from the second and third quarters of the eighteenth century. The final chapter will touch on the life-styles of the other people living in town during this period. For those readers interested in decorative arts and the material world of our ancestors, this book will give a sense of how curators today set about re-creating the eighteenth-century home environment and what it reveals about these people in history. This book will also provide the museum professional with a basic methodology that can be useful when furnishing historic houses, whatever their period.

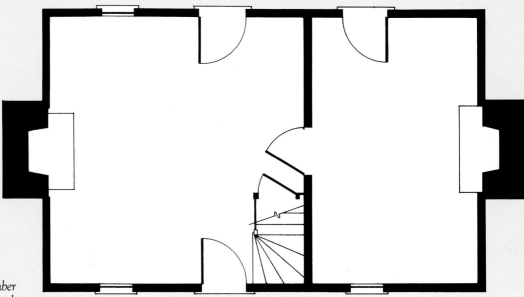

Fig. 11

Floor Plan of a Hall/Chamber House. Early in the eighteenth century many Virginia houses were constructed with this simple floor plan. Two rooms below and perhaps one or two above served the needs of colonists beginning a new life in the colony.

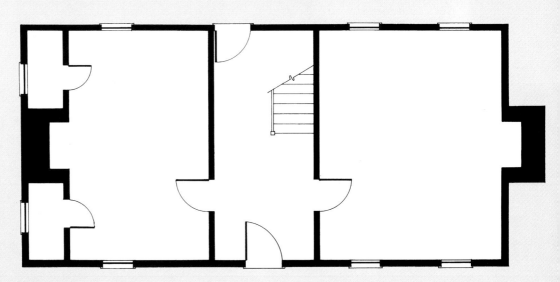

Fig. 12

Floor Plan of a Hall/Passage/Parlor House. As Virginians settled into their life here and increased their wealth, some chose to build larger, more impressive houses. With the partitioning of space, room usage became specialized, although in this period rarely exclusive to one activity.

The Parlor:
To Receive and Entertain

This tour of the eighteenth-century house begins with the parlor because its predecessor, the hall, was the primary living space of the house until the middle of the eighteenth century. Early in the eighteenth century, visitors entered the house at the front door, which opened directly into the hall (fig. 11). Here the owner, his family, servants, and guests lived, dined, drank, socialized, and frequently slept. As the century progressed, individuals felt a greater need for privacy and formality in their houses. Thus they partitioned off one end of the hall to create a corridor or passage as seen in figure 12. A visitor no longer entered immediately into the heart of a planter's house. Rather, he first entered the passage where he could be scrutinized and judged before being admitted to the hall. Later, as the dining room (across the passage from the hall) began to assume a more important social role, the hall became known as the parlor, which gave the space a more fashionable connotation. The reworking of space in the typical Virginia house plan was chiefly confined to well-to-do households where entertaining and impressions were of primary importance. Despite these changes, by the end of the eighteenth century inventories continued to refer to this space as a hall rather than a parlor.[1]

As dining increasingly took place in the dining room, other social activities such as musical entertainment, card playing, and tea drinking remained the primary activities that took place in the parlor. The type of furnishings characteristic of a fashionable parlor and appropriate for the function of entertaining are featured in a portrait of an Irish family painted about 1770 (fig. 13). A row of chairs stands against the wall on the left-hand side of the room, and only the furniture in actual use is

Fig. 13

An Irish Family Attributed to Philip Hussey. Oil on canvas. Ireland, ca. 1750. This conversation piece depicts the family in an elegant setting that was often the site of gatherings with guests. The size, elegance, and furnishings of the space indicate the owner's desire to show off the room to his peers. Courtesy, National Gallery of Ireland.

Fig. 14

George Wythe House Parlor. In the wintertime the parlor is furnished with a Turkish Ushak carpet. Despite the lack of an inventory, we know from the account of the sale of Governor Fauquier's estate that George Wythe owned a "Turkey" carpet that he purchased from Fauquier's estate. When the room was in use, the furniture was generally placed on the carpet.

brought into the center. The chair seats are covered in horsehair held in place with brass tacks. A carpet lies on the floor, and paper in the "pillar-and-arch" pattern adorns the walls. On the right between two windows hangs a looking or pier glass. The fireplace is fitted up with a modern coal grate, and on either side paired fire screens protect individuals from the excessive heat of the fire.

Many furnishing elements of this Irish interior are reflected in a view of the Wythe House parlor (fig. 14). The chairs not in use are lined up against the wall along with the tea and card tables. A period carpet on the floor adds color and warmth to the room. To the left between the windows hangs an English looking glass. In summer the Wythe parlor assumes a different look as seen in figure 15. The carpet has been taken up and the chairs covered with fitted check cases designed to protect them from dust and flies that were particularly troublesome in this season due to the open windows. The chairs and table needed for tea have been brought to the center of the room while the remaining furniture lines the walls, leaving room for the guests to move about.

These seasonal variations appear to have had their beginnings in English customs that Virginians increasingly adopted as the century progressed, possibly due in part to the increase in the availability of consumer goods which was on the rise in the second half of the eighteenth century. An examination of Lord Botetourt's inventory indicates such seasonal housekeeping practices, but further research needs to be done to determine the extent to which such English practices made their way into Virginia households. By the nineteenth century diaries and housekeeping manuals reveal that seasonal changes in furnishings had become an important part of the yearly household operations.

Although check covers might be used only seasonally, they were considered fashionable and could cover year-round, as the 1770 inventory of the Governor's Palace suggests. In the Middle Room on the second floor stood "8 Crimson damask chairs with red check covers,"[2] which protected the expensive damask upholstery from wear and fading and

Fig. 15

George Wythe House Parlor. The same parlor takes on a different look in the summertime with the addition of case covers on the chairs and the absence of the carpet. Although the appearance of the room changes, the function remains the same. The bare floor and the green and white check covers help create a cooler setting in which Mrs. Wythe can enjoy tea with a neighbor on a warm summer day.

Fig. 16

Governor's Palace Middle Room Upstairs. Covers today are often used to hide old chairs, but in the eighteenth century they more often served to protect the expensive upholstery underneath. The red check material was fashionable in the period and so was highly appropriate for a representative of the king.

Fig. 17

George, Prince of Wales, and Prince Frederick, later Duke of York, by Johann Zoffany. Oil on canvas. England, ca. 1765. The case covers in this scene are a more elegant version of the check covers. Here the covers are en suite with the wall covering, and probably the original upholstery as well. These covers served the same purpose as other covers—to protect from light and dust. Courtesy, Her Majesty the Queen.

Fig. 18

A Gentleman at Breakfast Attributed to Henry Walton. Oil on canvas. England, ca. 1775-1780. While the man and his dog are the focus of the painting, note the other furniture in the room that has obviously just been pulled out and used. To those concerned with material culture, the highly detailed background is also of interest. The attention to the particulars of the chair cases and the carpet give evidence of these features in a period setting. Courtesy, Toledo Museum of Art.

probably were removed only on formal occasions (fig. 16). In the painting by Johann Zoffany of a sitting room in Buckingham House in 1764, the furniture remains encased in loose covers even though the sitters are sons of George III, evidence that the royal family considered the covers suitable furnishings (fig. 17).

In another eighteenth-century painting, a provincial gentleman sits in a well-appointed room with tea equipment at hand (fig. 18). Note the carpet, the fire screen (which because of its four legs was called a "Horse-Fire-screen" in Thomas Chippendale's *Director*), and the check covers on the chairs. These covers served as prototypes for those in the Wythe parlor, while the wall-to-wall carpet provided evidence for laying the reproduction carpet in the Brush-Everard House parlor (fig. 19). Nail holes around the edges of the parlor floor contained eighteenth-century nail shanks. They indicated that wall-to-wall carpet had been a period feature and appropriate for this room. The Wilton carpet is a

Fig. 19

Brush-Everard House Parlor. Wilton carpeting had several advantages as a floor covering. It was ideal for a wall-to-wall carpet because it could be easily shaped to the size of the room and cut to fit around corners and fireplaces. It wore well, was cheaper than Turkey carpets, and could be made to order in any design, color, and size.

reproduction of a carpet designed by the renowned architect Robert Adam for Sir Lawrence Dundas in the mid-1760s. As with the original, the reproduction was woven in a twenty-seven-inch width, widths of the required length then being sewn together to form the desired size. Wilton carpeting could also be made into smaller area carpets like the reproduction installed in the parlor of the Peyton Randolph House. The same design as seen in figure 19 constitutes the center section of the carpet in figure 20, which is bound with a suitable border.

Fig. 20

Peyton Randolph House Parlor Carpet. The center of the carpet was a popular eighteenth-century pattern inspired by classical motifs. The original created for Sir Lawrence Dundas was intended as "a Wilton Roman Pavement Carpitt to fitt all round the bed with a Boarder on the outside." Its use at Colonial Williamsburg in two houses demonstrates the versatility of the period carpeting.

16

Fig. 21

A Family Being Served Tea. British school. Oil on canvas. England, ca. 1740–1745. As a servant brings in hot water, tea is being served to the family while one of the ladies plays a tune on the instrument, some of the activities that family and visitors enjoyed while sitting in the parlor. Philip Vickers Fithian, tutor to the children of Robert Carter at Nomini Hall plantation, noted in his Diary that on January 1, 1774, "the Colonel [was] in the Parlour tuning his Guitar." Courtesy, Yale Center for British Art, Paul Mellon Collection.

Fig. 22

The Game at Quadrille From an Original Painting in Vauxhall Gardens. Hand-colored line engraving. England, ca. 1750. Card games were very popular in the eighteenth century. Both men and women enjoyed the pastime, which often took place in the parlor and might be accompanied by tea. Robert "King" Carter on January 1, 1727/8, "sat most of the day there [and] plaid at cards." 1962-232, 3.

17

Fig. 23

Brush-Everard House Parlor. The time of day represented at this house is early in the morning. The parlor still shows signs of the previous evening's musical entertainment. The servant is just beginning to straighten up the room by collecting the ashes from the fireplace. Afterward he will put the furniture back against the walls.

The furnishings in the Brush-Everard House parlor are arranged to reflect the varied activities carried out in such a space (figs. 21, 22, 23, and 24). A square piano and guitar are evidence of an evening's musical entertainment with other chairs set around suggesting the presence of an audience. The room also contains a card table at which the guests could indulge in a game of loo or some other popular card game.

Estate inventories for Thomas Everard and George Wythe do not survive. In such cases composite lists of furnishings were created for the residences of the two men, based on the study of comparable Virginia inventories of the period. By examining the estate inventories of individuals whose social, economic, and political standing were similar to Everard and Wythe, we can deduce how their parlors probably were furnished.

The same method was applied at the Benjamin Powell and the James Geddy houses, two properties that reflect the life-style of the middling class. Basic furnishings of most parlors consisted of a set of chairs and a number of different tables to accommodate the various

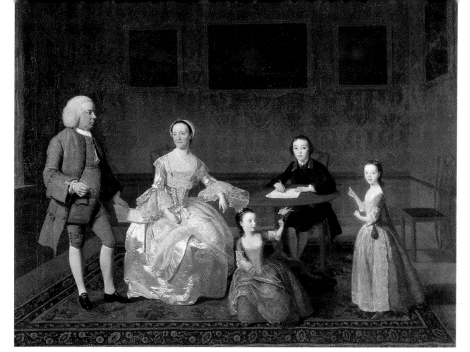

functions carried on in the room. The distinction between the upper and
middling houses is determined not so much by the type of furnishings as
by their quality. A typical entry for a well-to-do parlor is in the inventory
of the goods of the merchant William Hunter of Williamsburg who died
in 1761[3] (fig. 25). A less well-to-do individual might have had many of
the same items, but of lower value.

By the second half of the eighteenth century the central passage
often contained typical furnishings such as a set of chairs of lesser quality
that could easily be carried to other rooms (fig. 26). For example, Peyton
Randolph seems to have kept six mahogany chairs in the entry in his
house that were worth only about one-fifth of the set he used in his parlor.
Although they were of lesser value, chairs from the passage provided
appropriate additional seating in any room of the house. Windsor chairs

Fig. 25

*Inventory of William Hunter.
Most of these furnishings were
commonly found in eighteenth-
century parlors. Only the large
number of prints and the expensive looking glasses are atypical.
With the chairs and tables,
Hunter created a space to entertain his guests with tea and cards
in an elegant setting.*

79

un ers ?
app v :

Appraisment of the Estate of William Hunter Esquire dec. 24th August 1761

In the Parlour

2 Large Looking Glasses	£10
1 Chimney Glass with Sconces	5
1 Grate Fender Tongs Shovel and Bellows with a Poker	5 u 10
12 Mahogany Chairs two of them Arm'd	20
1 Square Maho. Table . £4 — 2 Card Tables £5 - 1 Round Table £1.15.	10 u 15
1 Tea Chest. 18/ 1 Large Carpet £4 - 1 Sea piece in a gilt Frame 15/.	5 u 13
14 Prints with Glass in Frames £3 — 1 Fire Screen £1.10 .	4 u 10

Fig. 26

Mr. and Mrs. Hayward by Sir William Beechey. Oil on canvas. England, ca. 1785. Passages are rarely pictured in paintings and prints, yet they are often described in written sources. This painting of the Hayward family offers a glimpse of the passage furnished with at least a table and painting. Courtesy, Christie's, London.

Fig. 27

Benjamin Powell House Passage. "[W]e took our seats in a cool passage where the Company were sitting," Fithian wrote in July 1774. Other Virginians noted making use of this space for reading, conversation, and occasionally for the children to recite lessons to the parents. It became more than just a way through to other rooms of the house. Here Mrs. Powell and her daughters make use of the space for sewing and music.

Fig. 28

George Wythe House Passage. Chairs line the wall of the passage where they are easily accessible for use in the dining room or parlor if extra seating should be needed.

like those illustrated in the photograph of the Benjamin Powell House began to appear in the passage from about 1760 onward (fig. 27). The chairs could be used when a group gathered in the passage to take advantage of "an air-draft in summer," for example, or could be taken outside where their green paint ideally blended into the garden or landscape.[4]

Tables often described in inventories as "old" or "round," the style popular early in the century and therefore old-fashioned by the 1760s and 1770s, were frequently placed in passages. Tables, centrally located in passages, could be transported to any room in the house when needed (fig. 28). To protect the floorboards of the passage from excess traffic or to keep rain, mud, or sand from being tracked into the house, a painted canvas floorcloth could be installed. One seems to have been in Peyton

Randolph's house. Couches, books, looking glasses and even a bed were occasionally found in the passage.

The creation of a passage separating the parlor from the door and from the other first-floor rooms more clearly defined a Virginian's sense of his public and private world. Along with the dining room, the parlor and passage were the rooms in which the gentry interacted with others in their society while surrounded by evidence of their taste and status. While these room divisions have been modified somewhat in the twentieth century, most traditional houses today still employ a passage or stylized entry hall as a buffer between the outside world and those people welcomed into the owner's house. Notions of formality have changed in the intervening two hundred years, but the idea of maintaining public rooms for visitors and private rooms for family still guides modern house design.

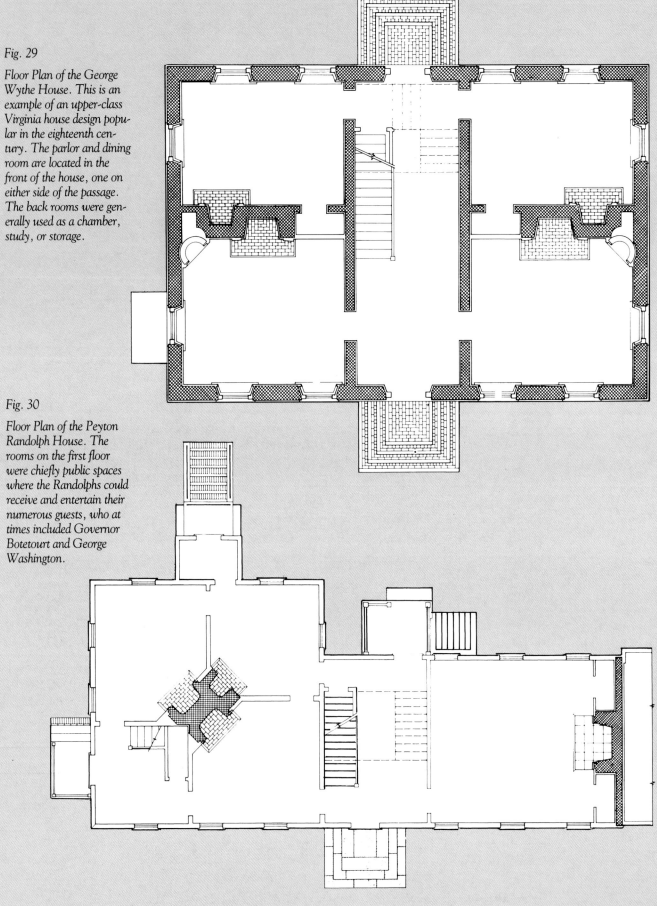

Fig. 29

Floor Plan of the George Wythe House. This is an example of an upper-class Virginia house design popular in the eighteenth century. The parlor and dining room are located in the front of the house, one on either side of the passage. The back rooms were generally used as a chamber, study, or storage.

Fig. 30

Floor Plan of the Peyton Randolph House. The rooms on the first floor were chiefly public spaces where the Randolphs could receive and entertain their numerous guests, who at times included Governor Botetourt and George Washington.

The Dining Room:
To Dine in Style

While the parlor served as a setting for cards and tea, the dining room was given over to the formal event of dining. The architectural space termed a dining room came into use about 1725, and by about mid-century it conformed approximately to our modern concept and use of such a space (fig. 31). In the second half of the eighteenth century, the "dining room was always one of the best and biggest rooms" in the grander houses of England.[5] The dining room in Virginia had also achieved a relatively comparable degree of importance, even though its evolution differed from that of the English prototype.

As the eighteenth century progressed the Virginia gentry moved individual functions out of their traditional multipurpose halls into more private spaces. The dining room became one of the most important and ceremonial of these new, separate rooms (fig. 29). By around 1750, the hall or parlor, dining room, and passage had evolved into three distinct but related social spaces—"the public component of the planter's domestic world."[6]

This development characterized urban dwellings as well as rural planters' houses—the Peyton Randolph House being a good example. The original section of the Randolph house was built circa 1715 and consisted of four rooms on each of the two floors. By the mid-1750s the house had been enlarged with a two-story addition that included a large dining room on the first floor[7] (fig. 30). While the parlor was furnished with some of the most expensive pieces in the house, the dining room was the largest in size and its architectural embellishment reflected its importance as the

Fig. 31

A Master Parson with a Good Living. Hand-colored line engraving. England, ca. 1760. This is a companion print to figure 38. In these prints, differences between upper- and lower-class households are readily apparent. Courtesy, the British Museum.

space devoted to dining, dancing, and musical diversions. The room's contents—enumerated in Peyton Randolph's estate inventory of 1776—complemented the social importance of the space:

12 Mahogany Chairs £15. 2 Mahogany tables £8	£23. 0.0
1 Card Table £2. 1 Marble Table £2	4. 0.0
1 Side Board Table 20/ 1 Carpet 20/	2. 0.0
4 looking Glasses £20 1 pr. End irons £2	22.0.0

In addition, over 250 pieces of china and glass ranging from plates to custard cups to water glasses were listed, as were 492 ounces of silver, for a grand total of £276. 7. 0.[8] The ceramics, glass, and silver were stored in bowfats—what today are referred to as closets—set into the wall on either side of the fireplace (fig. 32).

The furnishings displayed in the Randolphs' dining room are comparable to those of many other Virginia upper-class houses of the period. A print entitled "The Dinner" depicts an English meal being served in the 1770s and gives an idea of how Peyton Randolph's room appeared at dinner, the main meal of the day that was served at two or three o'clock in the afternoon (fig. 33). Seven diners are seated at the table while a butler and two waiters in livery see to their needs. During the meal the butler can dispense wine from a sideboard table against the

Fig. 32

Peyton Randolph House Dining Room. One of the two closets flanking the fireplace can be seen behind the diners. The closets provided a place for the storage of the numerous ceramics, glass, and silver owned by Peyton Randolph. The diners are enjoying the final course of dinner, which consisted of fruits and nuts and was served after the dessert course at which time the tablecloth was removed.

Fig. 33

The Dinner: Symptoms of Eating & Drinking. Colored stipple engraving. England, March 5, 1794. This print illustrates not only furnishings appropriate to the dining room but also the foods and how they were served. In the historic buildings in recent years an effort has been made to create accurate displays of eighteenth-century meals using both artificial and real food. 1954-698.

Fig. 34

Peyton Randolph House Dining Room. "Half after eight we were rung in to Supper; The room looked luminous and splendid; four very large candles burning on the table where we supp'd, three others in different parts of the Room; a gay, sociable Assembly, and four well instructed waiters!" Fithian reported in December 1773 while residing at Nomini Hall as tutor. Mr. Randolph's guests might have had a similar experience when they dined at his house.

Fig. 35

Charles at Breakfast in a genteel private Family. Line engraving. England, 1787. Despite the evolution of both a dining room and a parlor in the same house, the uses of the rooms varied. They were often furnished with a comparable number of chairs and both had tables. Parlors, though, generally had tables designated for tea or cards, as opposed to tables that were large enough to seat many people comfortably for dinner. 1959-83, 3.

wall. Hanging above are three sporting prints of a kind often found in the dining room. A delightful description of the dining room at Mount Airy in Virginia's Northern Neck in 1774 itemized "twenty four of the most celebrated among the English Race-Horses, Drawn masterly, and set in elegant gilt Frames."[9]

The evening meal, supper, was served about nine o'clock in eighteenth-century Virginia. In the dining room two tables have been joined together in order to accommodate a large group of guests at a formal supper (fig. 34). After some entertainment or conversation in the parlor, the guests were invited into the dining room to partake of a meal that featured meats and sweets. Against the wall on the right stand marble and sideboard tables similar to the kind listed in the inventory, while on the wall above hang two of the four looking glasses also called for in the inventory listings for this room.

In figure 35 a breakfast is being served in what is probably a parlor. This meal generally took place about eight or nine o'clock in the morning. A variety of beverages and foods could be served including chocolate, coffee, some types of hot breads, cakes, and cold meats (possibly remains from the evening before). All of these meals could be served formally in the dining room with all the proper equipment or less formally in other areas of the house.

Fig. 36

Governor's Palace Dining Room. The multipurpose use of rooms is exemplified here with the presence of a desk and library table in the dining area. These pieces, when inventoried in 1770, contained "sundry papers private and public" of the governor, indicating he attended to his business in this room.

Despite the fact that the inventories of many houses list both a dining room and parlor, room usage in eighteenth-century houses was often quite flexible and variable. Specific events like dining were not confined to one space in the house. Chairs and tables were relatively portable and could be moved to any part of the house as needed. And the needs could vary according to the time of day, the season, or any other circumstance. If there were a warm fire in the parlor in the dead of winter, for example, why leave that room and walk through an unheated passage into a room used only for eating? Why not stay warm in the parlor and have a table brought to you? The same situation could be true for the dining room. If one started the day with breakfast in the dining room, why leave its warmth merely to sit properly in the parlor? Desks and bookcases are not infrequently found in dining room contexts in Virginia inventories of the period, suggesting that the occupants could attend to business in the room when it was not being used for dining (fig. 36). One eighteenth-century Virginia diarist actually described the dining room as the "Room where we usually sit"[10] to enjoy conversation as well as business.

Figure 35, whether of a parlor or dining room, is important for the details it shows about dining customs. Covering the table is a cloth upon which is placed a tray with the tea service (mostly china) and a tea kitchen, an urn containing hot water ready to be poured into the teapot. A fashionable looking glass hangs on the wall and a handsome carpet

Fig. 37

Governor's Palace Dining Room. When curtains were used in spaces such as this, they might be seasonal. At the Palace the curtains are hung only in the winter to provide extra protection from cold drafts. The curtains, having been taken down for the summer and not yet rehung, were still stored in a closet when the inventory was taken in October 1770.

Fig. 38

*A Journeyman Parson with a Bare Exis-
tence. Colored mezzotint. England, ca.
1760.* Although the parson uses a tablecloth
on his table, the room in which he is eating is
probably the only room, or one of two
rooms, in the house. All activity, not just
dining, must take place in this same area.
While this print is satirical and not precisely
representational, it presents an idea of the
way many poorer families lived. 1971-476.

Fig. 39

*Tasting. Hand-colored line engraving.
England, 1784.* In a tavern context such as
this, the diners consisted only of men. Women
did not usually frequent taverns. Despite the
absence of women, the meal service closely
resembled that which took place in the home.
1964-472, 4.

Fig. 40

Raleigh Tavern Daphne Room. We can imagine a meal like the one pictured in figure 39 taking place in this private room.

covers the floor. Both items were characteristic of elegant dining rooms of this period. However, note that the windows have no curtains, since curtains were uncommon in such rooms. The Governor's Palace dining room, on the other hand, is provided with window curtains because the 1770 inventory of the building's contents describes them[11] (fig. 37). The royal governor at that time was an English lord, well able to afford such an expensive item; less affluent householders could not, or chose not to. Only in the next century did window curtains begin to appear in Virginia dining rooms with regularity.

Table linens were another matter. Regardless of how humble the house might be, a tablecloth appears to have been a necessity for the individual with any pretension to gentility. A print of a "Journeyman Parson" shows a clergyman who covers his table with a cloth despite his obvious poverty (fig. 38). At the other end of the economic scale, Peyton Randolph owned forty-eight tablecloths while Lord Botetourt at the Governor's Palace kept a wide variety of cloths including "30 Dinner table cloths," "4 Damask long Dinner table cloths," "4 long Diaper table cloths," and "36 Breakfast cloths," a clear testimony to their owner's important social rank.[12]

Large numbers of table linens appear frequently in tavern contexts as well. This is surprising until one understands that tavern keepers made money by serving special meals in private dining rooms. The print entitled "Tasting" shows such a dinner being served at an English tavern. The Raleigh Tavern and Wetherburn's Tavern in Williamsburg were equally equipped to provide these services to their colonial clientele (fig. 39). The "Daphne Room" was one of several rooms at the Raleigh Tavern available for a private dinner such as illustrated here, with all the linen, silver, ceramics, and glassware required to set an elegant table[13] (fig. 40). Comparable services were offered at Henry Wetherburn's Tavern where the "Great Room" could be rented for larger gatherings such as lectures and

Fig. 41

Wetherburn's Tavern Bull Head Room. This is one of the private rooms offered by Mr. Wetherburn for an extra fee. A group of gentlemen could rent the space in order to have a private game of cards or for other diversions. In the background we can see the evidence of Mr. Wetherburn's successful business in the form of such expensive items as the clock, prints, and pieces of silver.

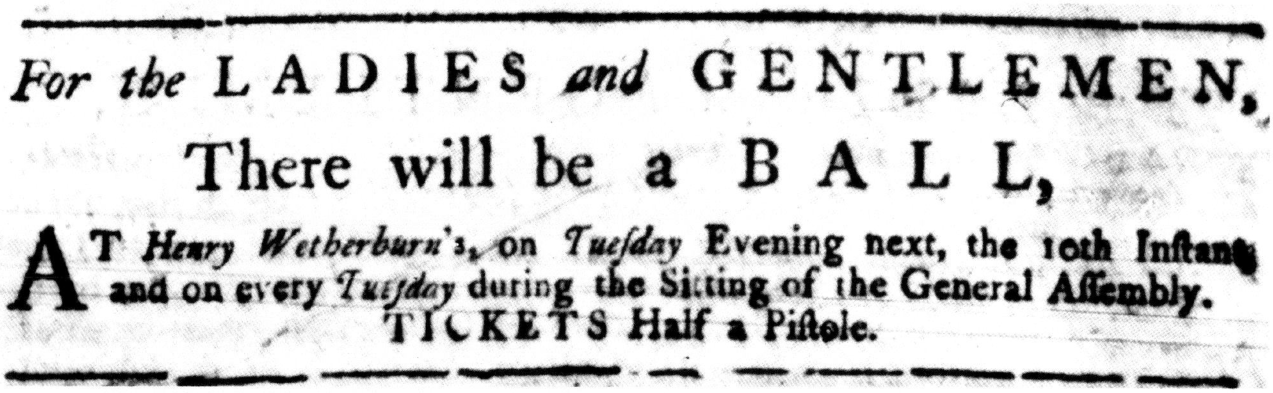

For the LADIES *and* GENTLEMEN,

There will be a BALL,

AT *Henry Wetherburn's,* on *Tuesday* Evening next, the 10th Instant, and on every *Tuesday* during the Sitting of the General Assembly.
TICKETS Half a Pistole.

Fig. 42

Virginia Gazette *Advertisement. The Great Room at Wetherburn's Tavern could accommodate a large group of people because of its size and numerous furnishings. Women were invited to dance and sup at the tavern during events such as an assembly.*

assemblies, while the "Bull Head Room" might be hired for more intimate occasions (figs. 41 and 42).

Although dining in the eighteenth century was generally a more self-conscious ritual than it is today, we see hints of its former importance on such special occasions as state banquets for heads of governments. At these ritualized functions, we perceive remnants of the protocol and formality that characterized eighteenth-century dinners, even down to the toasts that end the meal. And while the great majority of twentieth-century diners rarely participate in such formalized occasions, many adhere to the traditional notions of a home having a separate dining room, an idea that first developed in this country over 250 years ago.

Fig. 43

The Old Free Method of Rouzing a Brother Sportsman. Line engraving. England, 1755-1760. Despite the activity occurring in the room, the high-post bedstead dominates the background. Expensive high-post beds such as this one featured an elaborate cornice and a complete set of bed hangings. 1967-327.

The Bedchamber:
To Dress and Sleep

In the eighteenth century the first floor of some upper-class Virginia houses consisted of two public rooms, the parlor and dining room, and a more private space, the bedchamber. Compared with other bedchambers in the house, the chamber downstairs usually contained the more expensive furnishings which suggests that the master and mistress of the house occupied this space. In other Virginia houses all bedchambers were relegated to the upper floors, although a hierarchy in terms of furnishings still determined the importance of the sleeping arrangements. The rooms upstairs composed a series of bedchambers for guests and other family members. Most of these upper-class houses of the period contained at least two or three bedchambers; some even more.

The term bedchamber was in common use in England by the early seventeenth century. It denoted a room used mainly for sleeping in contrast to the bedchamber's earlier use as a multipurpose or bed-sitting-room.[14] In Virginia, however, the word chamber was generally used without the prefix bed, although such designations as room color or location—"white," "green," "back," "upper," or "hall"—occasionally precede "chamber" in early documents. The term "bedchamber" becomes more common after about 1770 in Virginia, which perhaps reflects a narrowing of the room's functions.

By the third quarter of the eighteenth century, the bedchamber was usually dominated by one or two bedsteads, sometimes because of a bedstead's sheer size, and at others because of its elaborate appearance (fig. 43). The bed (referring to what we would today call a mattress) and the

Fig. 44

Frederick arrested for Debt, and thrown in Prison. Line engraving. England, August 31, 1787. Low-post beds provided additional sleeping space in a room with a high post or were used alone or in pairs in secondary chambers. These beds can be detected in inventories because of their lower value and absence of curtains. 1959-83, 10.

Fig. 45

Brush-Everard House North-west Bedchamber. Like other high-post beds, the camp or field bed has a full complement of bed textiles. There is no elaborate cornice on this bed since the bed frame is covered entirely with fabric. Thus it is easier to disassemble and transport. The name comes from the military examples that could be taken down easily and carried in the field.

bedstead (meaning the wooden bed frame) along with the accompanying bed furniture including sheets, blankets, and bolster were normally placed in chambers rather than in public rooms like the parlor or dining room as had been the custom earlier. Bedsteads in affluent households were generally a combination of high post and low post (figs. 44 and 45). Low-post bedsteads can usually be identified in period inventories because there is no corresponding mention of curtains, curtain rods, or valances, the items necessary to dress out a high-post, camp, or field bed.

A bedstead might have one bed and one mattress on it, the lower mattress being filled with a coarse material such as wool flock, straw, even tow or marsh grass, while the upper bed was often made up of a soft material like curled animal's hair or feathers (see glossary). The beds lie on

Fig. 46

George Wythe House Chamber over the Dining Room. Because of its curtains and valances, a high-post bed was more difficult to set up than low-post beds. The upholsterer brought his tools to the house and fitted out the bed by nailing the valances to the frame and hanging the curtains on the rods.

Fig. 47

Plate XLIV (XXVII, 1st ed.) from Thomas Chippendale's The Gentleman and Cabinet-maker's Director. This plate shows a period drawing of pulleys similar to those on the governor's bed. As the bed was lacking its original cornice, this cornice (B) was used as the model for the one reconstructed. Holes in the frame revealed the original placement of the cornice. Although an English publication, the Director is known from inventories to have been used in Virginia.

Fig. 48

Governor's Palace His Lordship's Bedchamber. This antique Virginia bedstead had original markings on it that when studied in conjunction with print sources helped us to recreate its appearance. The pulley-lath construction is one of the few surviving eighteenth-century examples. Holes in the posts indicated the size and placement of the cloak pins that were reproduced from period examples found in Williamsburg during excavations. These features revealed that the curtains were of a type with double swags, termed "double drapery."

ropes or a combination of ropes, hides, and coarse linen strung between the side rails of the bedstead. For slaves and other servants this bed, stuffed with straw, might be laid directly on the floor.

A high-post bedstead consisted of additional features not found on the low-post bedstead. A superstructure called a cornice was fitted over the four posts. The cornice might be of plain wood, carved, or covered with fabric en suite with the other bed textiles.[15] The tester, a light wooden frame covered with fabric, either plain or matching the other textiles, lay inside spanning the length and breadth of the cornice.

The bed textiles or furniture included bed curtains, valances, and coverlets. Curtains with metal rings sewn along the top edge were generally suspended from metal rods that hung along the top between the bedposts (fig. 46). To create an even more elaborate appearance, the curtains might have small rings sewn to the back in a curved line. A string would be threaded through these rings and into a lath with pulleys (fig. 47). When the string was pulled, the curtains draped elegantly and could be held in that position by securing the string around cloak pins that were attached to the bedpost (figs. 48 and 49).

Fig. 49

Account Book of Governor Botetourt. While in Virginia, Lord Botetourt ordered many items for the Palace, including such small items as "Curton" rings, cloak pins, curtain line and pulleys, all of which were necessary to outfit a high-post bed properly. Courtesy, the Duke of Beaufort.

				13
Fenton brought forward	32 . 5 . 9½	666	6 . 11½	
For 8 grose of Brass oves ----		― .16 .―		
For a grose of Curton rings --		― . 5 .―		
For a grose of polished D° ----		― . 9 .―		
For 8 grose of Studs --- ---		― . 5 . 6		
For 2 Doz. of Cloakpins ----		― . 8 .―		
For 6 Doz. of Brass Scrue hooks		― . 6 .―		
For one grose of 2 Inch Scrues -		― . 5 . 6		
For 3 grose of Curton line ---		1 .10 .―		
F 12 tossels - - - - -		― .13 .―		
For 3 Peices of treed --- ---		― . 7 . 6		
For 36 yards of strong worstedlin		2 . 5 .―		
For 36 yards of Silk ditto ---		4 . 1 .―		
For 2 grose of pullys ---		― .13 .―		
For half a grose of long pullys		― . 4 .―		
For a Venetian blind --- ---		1 . 9 .―		
For a large packing Case & a small D° ---- ---		― .15 .―		
Paid the freight & Expences putting on board ---		2 . 5 .―		
Fentons Bill Total --- ―			A9 . 8 . 3½	
Con° tocc' ---			7 15 15 3	

Fig. 50

High Life at Five in the Morning. Line and etched engraving. England, May 1, 1769. The occupant of the bed holds back the curtains to see what is happening in the room. The foot curtains are still drawn. 1973-260.

Fig. 51

Governor's Palace His Lordship's Bedchamber. The bed displays its summer mosquito curtains of green gauze. The heavier winter curtains which replace these in colder weather are made from the same chintz pattern as that of the other bed furniture. The wood cornice is covered in the same fabric as the curtains, a period practice discussed in Chippendale's work. Chintz was highly fashionable by the second half of the eighteenth century.

Curtains could be let down or pulled together at night to ensure privacy or to cope with such winter inconveniences as drafty rooms (fig. 50). In summer, mosquito curtains might be substituted for heavier curtains, as we see again on the governor's bed (fig. 51). These lighter curtains allowed air to circulate around the sleeper and provided protection from insects. Such barriers were needed since window screens with fine mesh wire had not yet been developed.

Suspended from the cornice, the valances concealed the curtain hardware. They could be nailed or tacked to the outer edge of the cornice. Elaborate beds sported additional inner valances, as illustrated in the second plate of Hogarth's "Before and After" series (fig. 52). A head curtain hung at the head of the bed and lower valances attached to the

Fig. 52

After by William Hogarth. Line engraving. England, 1736. Because of the attention to detail, this print provides a period document on which to base the knowledge of bed construction. The rod, rings, and valances are all clearly visible. Compare this with figure 46. 1972-409, 157.

Fig. 53

Governor's Palace Chamber over the Dining Room. This bed round is a reproduction of a 1767 design that Robert Adam made for Coventry House. It was woven in three strips and then pieced together in a U-shape. In 1752 Mrs. Delany, an Englishwoman, wrote that her evening's work was to complete a carpet "to go round my bed."

Fig. 54

The Story of Pamela, Plate 7. Line engraving. England, 1745. The bed is surrounded by a bed round similar to the one in figure 53. Note that the bed is fitted out with all the necessary accoutrements. 1968-280, 7.

sides and foot rails completed the assemblage. Because they required so much fabric, beds were among the most expensive items in eighteenth-century households.

Sheets, blankets, pillows and bolsters, and a quilt (coverlet or counterpane) were the utilitarian items needed to dress the bed. In a letter to his wife, a Virginia tutor described the bedding (probably for a low-post bed) provided in the colonies: "I have a verry fine feather bed under me, and a pair of sheets, a thin fold of a Blanket and a Cotton bed spread is all my bed cloaths, and I find them Just enough."[16] A small carpet or bed round might be placed next to the bed in well-to-do households. A bed round was designed to surround the bed on three sides without extending underneath it. Figures 53 and 54 illustrate a bed round installed in the chamber over the dining room at the Governor's Palace, and the same feature included in an eighteenth-century print.

While providing a place to sleep was the primary function of this room, other activities occurred here as well, as indicated by the presence of a variety of furnishings. Pieces like dressing tables and looking glasses were common in bedchambers. Unlike the English estate, a Virginia house rarely had a separate room for dressing; therefore, a colonial lady dressed in the bedchamber making use of the table and glass as seen in the print "Noon" (fig. 55). A dressing table could be covered with a "toilet" cover such as we see in a

Fig. 55

Noon. Hand-colored mezzotint engraving. England, 1758. On the table are toilet articles and a swing glass that could be adjusted to catch the changing light. 1950-711.

Fig. 56

Mrs. Abington in "The Way to Keep Him" by Johann Zoffany. Oil on canvas. England, 1768. While this portrait of the actress probably depicts a dressing room, some of the same furnishings were found in Virginia bedchambers. The dressing table and glass are covered with a white cloth; an easy chair is to the left. Courtesy, the National Trust, England (Egremont Collection, Petworth).

Fig. 57

Brush-Everard House Northwest Chamber. Using the print in figure 55 for guidance, the dressing table and the lady's actions can be re-created in an eighteenth-century manner. The various toilet articles adorning the table are period antiques that could have been used by a young lady readying herself for the day's activities.

Fig. 58

George Wythe House Southeast Bedchamber. Mrs. Wythe sits comfortably in the easy chair sewing on her needlework. When pulled up to the fireplace, the "wings" on the chair help keep drafts away from the sitter and retain the heat from the fire. The chair wears a case made from the same fabric as that of the bed textiles. The fire screen shields her face from the fire as she leans forward to work.

portrait of Mrs. Abington painted by Johann Zoffany in 1768 (fig. 56) and in an upstairs chamber at the Brush-Everard House (fig. 57). The dressing table and glass were placed in front of a window for maximum light. Dressing glasses varied in types.

Depending on the size of the room, other types of tables might occasionally be found in the bedchamber. They ranged from a small, square type to a tea table and provided a surface for a family member to work in private or informally entertain a few close friends.

Fig. 59

James Geddy House Bedchamber. James Geddy, a successful local craftsman, had a well-furnished house. In his bedchamber, though, are old-fashioned chairs from the 1720s. The cradle and toys indicate the presence of young children who might have slept or played in their parents' room. Clothing is stored in the clothespress.

43

Fig. 60

Brush-Everard House Mr. Everard's Chamber. This walnut clothespress has sliding shelves that give easier access to the folded clothing. Another form of this same type has a set of shelves in the top cabinet while the lower portion consists of a series of drawers.

Since a variety of activities took place in this space, seating furniture was also an important component of a bedchamber's furnishings. An easy chair, or what is today known as a wing chair, was frequently found here. Not only was this large chair comfortable, but it could also conveniently conceal a chamber pot, thereby transforming it into a closestool. An easy chair was a fairly expensive item due to the amount of textile and skilled labor needed to upholster the piece. One has been installed in the Wythes' bedchamber (fig. 58), while a similar chair can be seen to the left of the dressing table in the Zoffany painting (see fig. 56). A small number of side chairs might also have been kept in the chamber. Old, out-of-fashion parlor or dining room chairs often were relegated to a secondary space such as a bedchamber, as in the first-floor chamber at the James Geddy House, an example of a middling household (fig. 59).

As the bedchamber was a room in which the occupants not only slept but also dressed, a place was needed in which to store clothing. The eighteenth-century storage method primarily consisted of folding the apparel. Chests of drawers and clothespresses were used for this purpose. A clothespress, an eighteenth-century word for cupboard, was a large case piece outfitted with drawers or shelves on which clothes were laid. Doors hid clothing from view and protected it from dust (fig. 60). Occasionally clothespresses or chests of drawers were not listed in an inventory, for example in the case of the chamber over the dining room at the Peyton Randolph House. In this instance the clothes were probably stored in built-in closets flanking the fireplace (figs. 61 and 62). Clothing stored in a closet might be hung directly on pegs or folded and laid on shelves.

Fig. 61

Peyton Randolph Inventory. This listing of the contents of the Randolphs' bedchamber is typical of many eighteenth-century bedchambers. Standard furnishings consisted of one or more beds, a dressing table, and a few chairs.

Fig. 62

Peyton Randolph House Chamber over the Dining Room. One item missing from the Randolphs' list is a clothespress. Architectural evidence suggests that the closets on either side of the fireplace were equipped for clothing storage.

Fig. 63

Wetherburn's Tavern Room over the Middle Room. Not all lodgings were this elegant. This room, which could accommodate from three to five people, was rented by Henry Wetherburn to gentlemen who paid a little extra for better and more "private" conditions.

The bedchamber was a room in which members of the family could find privacy and rest, qualities that were certainly not characteristic of sleeping places in many taverns and inns. In those commercial establishments rooms for the public were generally not referred to as chambers; rather, they were rooms or lodgings.[17] Although some of the bedchamber furnishings noted above were enumerated in tavern inventories, the quantity and quality of the items often differed from those of the private home. Very seldom did tavern beds approach the value of beds in well-to-do houses. The most expensive bed in Wetherburn's Tavern, for example, one of Williamsburg's best commercial establishments, was about half the value of the most expensive bed at Peyton Randolph's house.[18] Yet the curtains, beds, and bedsteads in taverns were still quite similar *in form* to their counterparts in private dwellings (figs. 63 and 64).

Beds predominated among the furnishings of the lodging rooms in taverns. Tables and dressing glasses were placed in sleeping areas, but generally in quite limited quantities. Surprisingly, the number of chairs is also low when compared to the number commonly found in houses. In at least one instance, the Raleigh Tavern, no chairs were listed for the second floor where the commercial bedrooms were located. The Raleigh did have window curtains in at least one of its upstairs rooms[19] (fig. 65).

As noted earlier, window curtains, when they do appear in eighteenth-century inventories, are mentioned most frequently in bedchambers. Window curtains, as with bed textiles, could be of varying qualities and styles, but their primary function in a chamber context was to provide privacy for the room's occupants.

Bedchambers were more private, family-oriented, and less formal than the triad of public spaces. More so than today, family life revolved around this room. It was the scene of births, illness, and deaths. The bedchamber reflected increasing needs for privacy, not only within the household but also from the outside world. This sense of privacy has progressed from its eighteenth-century beginnings as an informal space for family gatherings to the current perception of bedrooms as an individual's refuge from others.

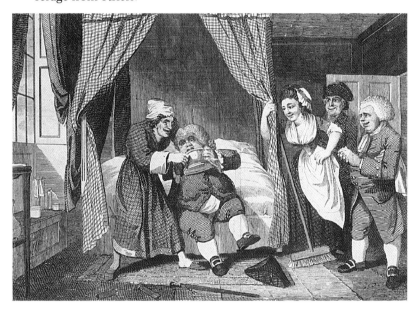

Fig. 64

The Patient's Paroxysm, or, the Doctor Outwitted. Engraving. England, 1784. This scene depicts the interior of a lodging in an English inn. The bed, like in domestic settings, is outfitted with curtains and upper and lower valances. This print shows one way of holding back the curtains—wrapping them around the bed post. Courtesy, the British Museum, Sir Ambrose Heal Collection.

Hay's Appraisement — Inventory and Appraisement of the Estate of Anthony Hay late of the City of Williamsburg Tavern keeper Deceased

	£	s	d
3 Bedsteads 30/. 3 Beds 3 Bolsters 3 Pillows 200/.	11	10	–
2 Matts 1 Hide 6/3. 1 pine Table 3/9	–	10	–
1 Bedstead, 1 Bed 1. Bolster 1 Pillow 1 Matt	4	10	–
1 Small Looking glass 7/6, 1 old Walnut Table 5/	–	12	6
1 Chest 10/. 1 Cloaths press 20/. 11 old prints (the Cavalry)	2	2	–
1 Bedstead and striped Holland Curtains. 1 Bed 1 Bolster 1 Pillow 1 Hide	7	–	–
1 Pine Table	–	3	9
2 Bedstead and red strip'd Curtains 2. Beds 2 Bolsters 2 pillows and 2 Hides	14	–	–
3 White Window Curtains 7/6, 1 pine Table 3/9	–	11	3
2 Bedsteads, 2 Matts, 2 Beds 2 pillows 2, Bolsters	8	–	–
1 Small Looking Glass 5/. 1 Fender and Poker 2/6, 1 Pine Table 3/9	–	11	3
2 Bedsteads and blue Check Curtains, 1 Hide, 2 Beds, 2 Bolsters 2 pillows	13	–	–
23 Chamberpots & 2 Basons 25/. 1 Pine Table 5/.	1	10	–
2 Bedsteads 2 Matts 2, Beds 2 pillows 2 Bolsters	7	–	–
1 Pine Table	–	5	–
1 Bedstead 1 Bed 1. Bolster 1 Pillow 80/ 1 Walnut Table 7/6	4	7	6
3 Bedsteads 2 Hides 3 Beds 3 Bolsters 3 Pillows 1. Matt	13	–	–
1 Table	–	3	9

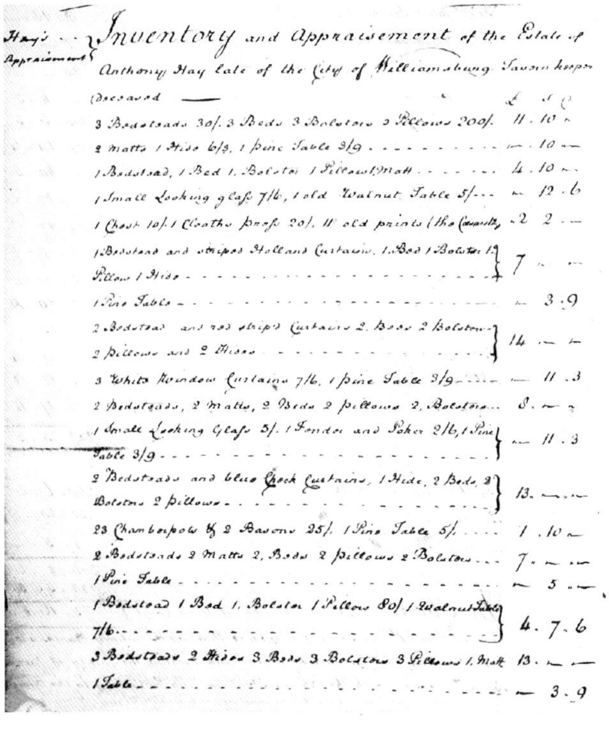

Fig. 65

Raleigh Tavern Inventory. This excerpt enumerates the typical furnishings for six of the tavern's lodgings, which differ little from those of a domestic bedchamber. Each room entry begins with the bedstead and ends with a table. Window curtains as listed here were probably hung in one of the more private rooms available at the Raleigh Tavern similar to that shown in the print above. Not all rooms offered a domestic atmosphere, however. "For company all the night in my Room I had Bugs in every part of my Bed—and in the next Room several noisy Fellows playing at Billiards," Fithian noted.

Fig. 66

*An Unknown Man in a Library by Arthur Devis. Oil on canvas. England,
1740-1741. In Virginia, men like Robert Carter collected books. Fithian
noted, "I was sitting in the Colonels Library I took a Catalogue of the whole
of His Books—and he tells me he has left behind him at Williamsburg, with
many other things 458 volumes besides Music and Pamphlets." Note the
decorative use made of the coal grate for summer. Courtesy, Yale Center
for British Art, Paul Mellon Collection.*

The Study:
To Nourish the Mind

The study was a space unique to the houses of the wealthier men of society. Because of its association with books and intellectual pursuits, the study was most appropriate for the educated people who had the time and money to devote to reading and thought. In the eighteenth century these educated individuals were usually gentlemen rather than ladies and members of the gentry rather than middling farmers (fig. 66).

Before the adoption of an entire room devoted to books, the English gentleman's collection of volumes (often called a library of books) was generally kept in the gentleman's closet adjoining his bedchamber, although some were found in the hall or bedchamber itself.[20] This pattern of storage was transplanted to Virginia. Small numbers of books were inventoried in halls or chambers throughout Virginia's first century of settlement while larger collections were kept in closets (fig. 67).

Although the study was a rare occurrence in many early Virginia houses of the seventeenth and eighteenth century, the presence of books in Virginia began with the formation of the colony itself when several volumes were transported to the southern colonies with the ill-fated Roanoke expedition of the 1580s.[21] The term "study" appears as early as 1655/6 in a Northampton County inventory, but the use made of this room in this period was not yet the private study of a gentleman and his

Fig. 67

Brush-Everard House Study. Thomas Everard, a wealthy gentleman, held several government positions including serving twice as mayor of Williamsburg. Although no inventory for his house exists, Everard's prominence in town suggests that he had a collection of books like the one pictured here. The titles in this library were compiled from a list made by Thomas Jefferson for a wealthy person of average intellectual pursuits. This room not only served as Everard's library and office, but also as a place to enjoy a family meal.

Fig. 68

Colonel William Byrd II by an artist in the studio of Sir Godfrey Kneller. Oil on canvas. England, 1700-1704. William Byrd II, a wealthy Virginia landowner, was educated in London. He amassed a collection of almost four thousand volumes, one of the largest libraries in the colony. In his diary Byrd recorded the time he spent organizing his library and showing it off to friends. 1956-561.

books.[22] For example, the inventory of Nathaniel Bradford's estate taken in 1690 lists a "Studdy" that contained a few books, but the other contents, which consisted of bottles, tools, and large quantities of sugar, fabric, and candles, suggest that this room was used more as a storage area than for reading and retirement.[23]

By the mid-eighteenth century studies were becoming more like their twentieth-century counterparts. By 1775 the formal definition recognized its primary importance as an "apartment set off for literary employment."[24] While today we commonly refer to such a space as a library, the term was not frequently used in this period.

Attempting to accurately re-create a study in one of the exhibition buildings is more difficult than furnishing the other rooms in a house because of the scarcity of sources. Like the dining room, this room was rarely depicted in prints and paintings. Other sources such as written accounts and architectural analysis make up, in part, for lack of pictorial representation, however. For example, a survey of period inventories and journals confirms that libraries of books were confined to the households of the elite. Further, rooms designated as studies were generally "the least of all first floor spaces"—least in terms of their size as well as their architectural embellishment[25] (fig. 69). This factor may be an evolutionary characteristic that is a holdover from libraries having been previously located in closets.

By the third quarter of the eighteenth century, studies had become a part of many Virginia gentry household plans—from Gunston Hall in northern Virginia to Menokin in the Northern Neck to the George Wythe House in Williamsburg, where Littleton Waller Tazewell recalled in his memoir that as a student he always found Mr. Wythe waiting for him "in his study by sunrise" (fig. 70). In Wythe's study was kept "his well stored library" for the use of students reading law and languages with him.[26]

Fig. 69

Floor Plan of Menokin, 1769. Home of the statesman Francis Lightfoot Lee, Menokin's plan called for a study to be the smallest room on the first floor. Against one wall is a press that most likely contained the library. Courtesy, the Virginia Historical Society.

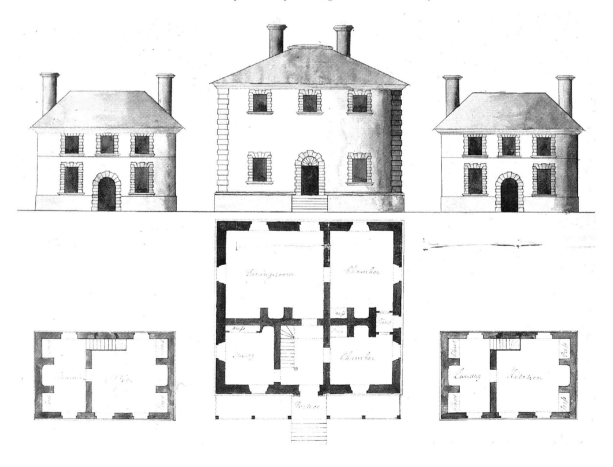

Fig. 70

George Wythe House Study. George Wythe, active in government, the law, and education, also found time to study a variety of subjects. He had an extensive library of books that contained works on Greek, Latin, law, religion, and many other topics.

Several of the houses in Williamsburg had rooms designated as studies, due in large part to the number of well-educated, wealthy gentlemen who chose to live here. Being the seat of government for the colony and the site of the college, the town naturally attracted such residents, including the governor. Lord Botetourt had a study at the Palace which adjoined his bedchamber (fig. 71). In this room were the following items that belonged to the governor:

> 1 Shovel, tongs, poker fender, hearth broom
>   Map of N. and S. America
> 20 Prints
> 1 blue venetian blind
> 1 Wilton carpet
>   Books as Pr Catalogue [over 300 volumes] with
>   the 2 Curtains which cover them
> 1 Japann'd ink stand, 1 green wax taper with
>   japann'd stand

Also in the room were "1 Looking Glass. 1 check Curtain and Rod [and] 1 Writing Table," all of which were the property of the colony of

Virginia.[27] A standard item for a study that is missing in this list is a
bookpress. The three hundred volumes owned by the governor were
probably stored on built-in bookshelves since this provided a proper place
for the books, but would not have appeared in the inventory because
architectural features were not valued. An illustration of a similar room in
England gives an idea of the way in which the two curtains listed in the
inventory in conjunction with the books were to be used (fig. 72). Since
books were valuable objects, it is understandable that measures were taken
to protect them from dust and light. An English print of about 1765 shows
another instance of this combination of a bookcase and curtain as well as

Fig. 72

Colonel Edmonstoun and Lord
Eliock by Alexander Nasmyth. Oil
on canvas. England, eighteenth century. Books were expensive items
and, as Susanna Whatman warned
her servants in the housekeeping book
that she wrote for their use in 1776,
"are not to be meddled with." Other
items of learning such as globes or
maps might also be found in the
study. Commenting on Robert
Carter's study, Fithian noted, "I
spent much of this Day in Mr Carters
Library among the works of mighty-
Men; I turned over Calmets, Scripture prints, they are beautiful, and
vastly entertaining." Courtesy, the
Marquess of Bute.

decorating features such as the map and two prints hanging on the walls (fig. 73). These furnishings are similar to what the governor would have had, but on a simpler scale.

Peyton Randolph, a lawyer and Speaker of the House of Burgesses, had an elegantly furnished house that contained a study. The 1776 inventory listed "a Library of Books as pr. Catalogue 250.0.0" made up of books Peyton inherited from his father, Sir John Randolph, as well as books acquired on his own. Even though the items in the inventory were not separated into individual rooms, it is possible to locate the furnishings for the study, which begin with "6 Mahogany Book presses at 30/" and continue with:

1 Do. Writing Table £3 1 large Mahogany table £5
1 Round table 15/ 1 paper press 10/
1 Chaffing dish 5/ 1 dry rubbing Brush 3/
1 Clock £5 1 pr. Back Gammon tables 10/

Fig. 74

Peyton Randolph House Study. Peyton Randolph's father not only left his son his library of books but also five mahogany bookpresses in which to store them. Upon Randolph's death many of these books were acquired by Jefferson for his library at Monticello. Eventually these books formed the basis of the Library of Congress.

Fig. 75

Lord Halifax and his Secretaries Attributed to Daniel Gardner, after Hugh Douglas Hamilton. Oil on canvas. England, ca. 1765-1767. Lord Halifax (in the right foreground) is dictating to one of his secretaries while another is using the candle to melt wax in order to seal a letter. This scene is typical of what might have occurred in an eighteenth-century study. Courtesy, National Portrait Gallery, London.

While the reason for the dry rubbing brush is an enigma, the other items are all obvious furnishings for a room in which Peyton Randolph kept his library, conducted his law practice, carried on his political business, and even entertained his gentlemen friends (figs. 74 and 75). The several tables provided the necessary surfaces on which to compose documents and spread out papers and books. The paper press in this room kept important documents from wrinkling while the backgammon tables suggest that the room was used for more relaxing pursuits than just those of a purely business nature. One interesting omission from the inventory for this room (which also is evident in the library of the Governor's Palace) is any type of seating furniture. However, a group of "6 old Chairs £3" are found in the room listed immediately before the study, and "6 Mahogany Chairs 40/" are indicated for the space directly after it.[28] Mr. Randolph probably used chairs from either of these spaces to provide seating in his study.

The furnishings listed above created a comfortable setting for both professional and pleasurable pursuits. While the eighteenth-century lady might entertain her guests in the parlor or her chamber, the gentleman could retreat with his friends to his study (fig. 76). This eighteenth-century use of the study is not unfamiliar to us today. While the furnishings have become more upholstered, the walls paneled in natural woods, and textiles cover the floor and hang at the windows, the study is still a retreat for those who wish to spend some quiet time alone with a favored book or friend.

Fig. 76

Charles concluding a Treaty of Marriage, with the Daughter of the Nobleman. Line engraving. England, 1787. One of a series, this print depicts the moment when Charles negotiates an important business deal—his marriage. Once the contract is signed, the gentlemen will relax, and possibly have something to drink to celebrate. Note the many books scattered on shelves and on the floor and the map hanging on the wall. 1959-83, 7.

Fig. 77

The Story of Pamela, Plate XII, by Joseph Highmore. Oil on canvas. England, 1744. When possible, a room's bed, chairs, and windows would be outfitted with matching textiles to create a unified appearance. Courtesy, The Syndics of the Fitzwilliam Museum, Cambridge, England.

The House:
To Fit Out and Adorn

In the previous four chapters we have looked at eighteenth-century domestic spaces by specific room and function. Each of these spaces has different furnishings and usages, yet each also has certain features in common such as windows and fireplaces. When the eighteenth-century occupant moved into his house, he was able to furnish each room according to his taste and his economic means. While a wife may have had some influence on how the house was decorated, the husband appears to us today as having been the decorator since it was he who ordered the goods and whose records survive. They had to decide how to dress the windows, decorate the walls, cover the floors, and treat the fireplace. These choices confront anyone faced with decorating an empty dwelling, whether that person be the eighteenth-century inhabitant or the twentieth-century curator.

Windows

Windows are an architectural feature common to all houses. Depending on the taste and wealth of the owner, they can be dressed in several ways. One window treatment available in the eighteenth century was venetian blinds. Although no period print sources depict these blinds, they appear in inventories and advertisements and their virtues are extolled in several written accounts. In England Susanna Whatman, writing a housekeeping book in 1776 for her servants, instructed the maid on how and when to adjust the blinds in the various rooms so that the furnishings would be protected from the sun.[29] In the advertisement from

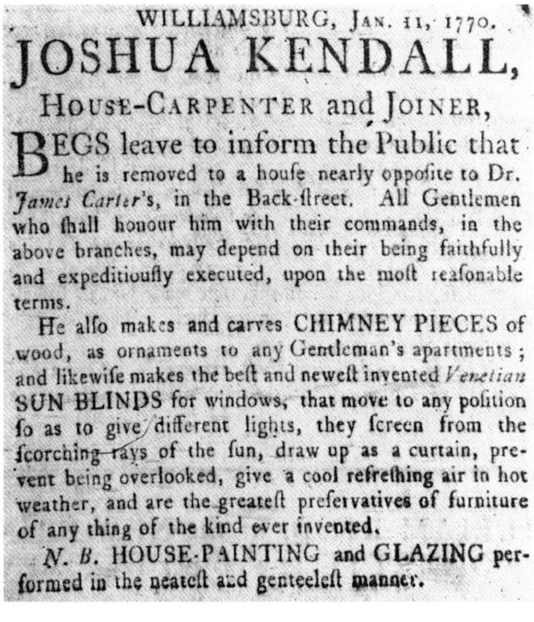

Fig. 78

Virginia Gazette, *January 18, 1770.*
Venetian blinds were used in the eighteenth century for much the same purposes that make them popular today. The blinds can be adjusted to admit a limited amount of light, thus preventing damage to the furnishings. They were made of wood and were usually painted green.

WILLIAMSBURG, Jan. 11, 1770.

JOSHUA KENDALL,

House-Carpenter and Joiner,

BEGS leave to inform the Public that he is removed to a house nearly opposite to Dr. *James Carter's,* in the Back-street. All Gentlemen who shall honour him with their commands, in the above branches, may depend on their being faithfully and expeditiously executed, upon the most reasonable terms.

He also makes and carves CHIMNEY PIECES of wood, as ornaments to any Gentleman's apartments; and likewise makes the best and newest invented *Venetian* SUN BLINDS for windows, that move to any position so as to give different lights, they screen from the scorching rays of the sun, draw up as a curtain, prevent being overlooked, give a cool refreshing air in hot weather, and are the greatest preservatives of furniture of any thing of the kind ever invented.

N. B. HOUSE-PAINTING and GLAZING performed in the neatest and genteelest manner.

Fig. 79

Paul Sandby by Francis Cotes. Oil on canvas. England, 1759. Shutters were recessed into the wall. Susanna Whatman warned her servants "to force back all the window shutters: otherwise they get warped, and will not go into their place which makes a room look very bad indeed." Courtesy, Tate Gallery, London.

the *Virginia Gazette* Mr. Kendall details the positive aspects of hanging window blinds (fig. 78). Blinds kept sunlight from striking and fading the furniture and allowed any breezes to cool the room especially in the summertime.

The thick walls of a house constructed of brick made it possible to have built-in shutters as an alternative to hanging window blinds as seen in this painting of the artist Paul Sandby (fig. 79). When the room was not in use, these solid paneled shutters could be closed to cover the windows completely (fig. 80). This gave protection from drafts and prevented the sun from damaging the room's furnishings. While the family occupied the space, the shutters could be opened fully or only partially to allow the desired amount of light into the room.

Another option was to decorate with curtains. Today curtains are hung in practically every room in the house, but in the eighteenth century they were found most frequently in bedchambers and only occasionally in other rooms such as the dining room.[30] In figure 77 the curtain is drawn

Fig. 80

George Wythe House Back Room. When closed, the solid shutters could be barred for added security. Shutters protected the rooms from excessive light. Susanna Whatman wrote, "The blinds will not always exclude it [the sun]. I am often obliged to shut the shudders."

Fig. 81

Lord Willoughby de Broke and his Family by Johann Zoffany. Oil on canvas. England, ca. 1770. Small metal curtain rings are attached to the window curtain with a cord threaded through them so that when pulled the curtain will drape in the fashion of those seen in the Governor's Palace dining room. Note also the carpet on the floor and the fire in the fireplace, all features suggesting winter. Courtesy, Thomas Agnew and Sons, Ltd., London.

Fig. 82

Brush-Everard House Mr. Everard's Chamber. The two windows in this first-floor bedchamber are fitted with curtains that match the bed textiles. Both the curtains at the window and those around the bed provided an extra degree of privacy for the occupant.

Fig. 83

Samuel Richardson by Joseph Highmore. Oil on canvas. England, 1750. The setting in which the author Richardson is depicted reveals that it is summertime as evidenced by the lack of carpet on the floor and the presence of a vase of flowers in place of andirons and a fire. Highmore became friends with Richardson while creating the illustrations for Pamela. Note the books behind the author and the presence of the curtain to protect them. Courtesy, National Portrait Gallery, London.

up in the Venetian style to create a ballooning effect and is of the same fabric as the curtains around the bed. The curtain in figure 81 has been let down and reveals the position of the attached rings and cord which, when pulled up, will cause the curtain to drape. This is the same method used on the high-post beds discussed in chapter three.

Curtains in the eighteenth century referred to both bed and window hangings, and thus window curtains can only be identified with

Fig. 84

Family Group by Charles Phillips. Oil on canvas. England, ca. 1730. Not all carpets covered the entire floor. When one sees a carpet in the room though, the activity is generally taking place in that space. 1936-190.

assurance if the reference specifically describes them as such (fig. 82). While English graphic sources show curtains in most rooms, not just the bedchamber, written documents reveal that this practice was not common in Virginia until the nineteenth century. This contradiction points out the inaccuracies that could occur if only one source is consulted. It is important to look at and compare as many types of evidence as are available.

Floors

The floors in most eighteenth-century Virginia houses (as well as in some English houses) were untreated pine boards (fig. 83). Many period housekeeping books give instructions on how to care for the bare floors, including dry rubbing, a process much like sanding. Dry herbs and sand were strewn on the floor and then rubbed well into the boards with a brush.[31]

Coverings were available, but it was not unusual for floors to be left bare, especially in the summer. Floor coverings of the period included Turkey carpets, Wilton carpets, or wall-to-wall carpeting (all discussed in chapter one) as seen in the Brush-Everard House. Figure 84 shows that Turkey carpets, which had appeared on tables earlier, were being used on the floor by the middle of the eighteenth century.

While carpets were elegant, they were expensive and hard to clean. A cheaper alternative was to lay down an "oyl" or floorcloth. A heavy piece of canvas was thickly painted, in a plain color, with its own unique design, or in imitation of marble (fig. 85). Floorcloths occur in inventories most commonly for passages and dining rooms. Since these cloths could be easily cleaned, they were well suited to areas that were bound to accumulate dirt from high usage.

Virginians could import floorcloths, although there was risk in doing so as Thomas Nelson discovered in 1773. His cloth arrived "injur'd by being role'd before the paint was dry."[32] The alternative was to purchase them from local craftsmen. Joseph Kidd, a Williamsburg upholsterer, advertised in the *Virginia Gazette* that he painted "floor cloths, chimney boards, and signs, according to directions."[33] He also repaired them, as the "oyl" cloth belonging in Lord Botetourt's dining room was listed in the inventory as being "at Mr Kids"[34] (fig. 86).

Seasonal conditions could affect when and where carpets and window curtains were to be used. Without central heating or air conditioning, the occupants had to find other ways to maintain a comfortable temperature in their houses. In winter curtains could be placed at windows and occasionally doors to help eliminate drafts. These curtains might remain year-round or be taken down in summer leaving the windows unadorned allowing for better air circulation. As for floors, many were left bare in summer, while in winter carpets helped to retain warmth.[35] This seasonal use of curtains and carpets applied only to those who chose to purchase these luxuries, so many Virginia houses were without such furnishings.

Fireplaces

Fireplaces, being a major source of heat and light especially in the winter, were found in almost every room of the house[36] (fig. 87). They were furnished with a pair of andirons to hold the wood in place or with a grate that was used for burning coal or wood. Some fireplaces were also equipped with an iron fireback that helped reflect heat into the room.

Fig. 87

Governor's Palace Parlor. While grates like this one were in use in the latter half of the eighteenth century, many Virginians still equipped the fireplace with andirons.

Fig. 88

Governor's Palace Middle
Room Upstairs. The chimney
board made of wide boards or
of canvas stretched on a
wooden frame was wedged
into the fireplace opening and
secured by a turnbuckle or
latch at the top. Some boards
were left plain while others
were wallpapered or painted
with scenes.

With the arrival of summer and warmer weather, fireplaces not used for
cooking might be emptied of the andirons or grates. The opening could be
filled with a large vase or a display of flowers, or the brass andirons or
grates, polished and emptied of wood or coal, would remain to decorate
the space (fig. 84). Another option was to close the fireplace completely
with a painted or wallpapered chimney board fitted to the size of the
opening (fig. 88). When Lord Botetourt's inventory was taken in October
1770, it was apparently cold enough to have already begun making fires
since the andirons and grates were listed in each of the downstairs rooms
and the chimney board for the dining room was put away in storage.[37]

Walls

The interior walls of a house could be plastered, papered, or painted.
Many rooms in Williamsburg houses are wainscoted, or paneled, below

Fig. 89

Brush-Everard House Dining
Room. The walls in this room were
wainscoted from the floor to the
chair rail and papered above. A reproduction based on a late eighteenth-century paper fragment
found in this room now covers the
walls in the room.

63

Fig. 90

Sir Lawrence Dundas and his Grandson in the Library at 19 Arlington Street, London by Johann Zoffany. Oil on canvas. England, 1769. The walls are covered with blue paper bordered by an intricate gilt strip. This painting was the basis for the paper and border hung in the ballroom of the Palace. Courtesy, the Marquess of Zetland.

Fig. 91

Governor's Palace Ballroom. In 1771 Robert Beverley noted that "Ld B had hung a room with plain blue paper and border'd it with a narrow stripe of Gilt Leather wch I thought had a pretty effect." Botetourt also intended to paper the Supper Room since in storage was listed "a long Box of Gilt bordering intended for the supper Room" as well as linen on which the paper would be pasted for the same room.

Fig. 92

Governor's Palace Parlor. The
inventory of 1770 listed as part of
the colony-owned furniture "34
Scripture Prints." While religious
themes were popular subjects for
prints, one of the most popular
artists in the medium was William
Hogarth who specialized in series
as well as individual prints depicting everyday eighteenth-century
life. Like many artists, Hogarth
painted the subject first and then a
printmaker created an engraving.

the chair rail and plastered above (fig. 89). Some rooms like the ballroom
at the Governor's Palace were also papered and trimmed with a gilt
border.[38] This treatment is very similar to that depicted in this painting
by Zoffany (figs. 90 and 91).

Once the finish of the wall was determined, the owner could then
choose to decorate the walls with paintings, frequently of family members,
and prints, sometimes a series or individual works by Hogarth. Some
unframed prints in areas with less expensive furnishings were treated with
varnish and then nailed directly to the wall. Framed material was often
hung with small brass rings and nails. The prints could be arranged singly
or in sets. For instance, in the Governor's Palace parlor there is a set of
thirty-four scripture prints that cover a good portion of the wall (fig. 92).
Other decorative and useful hangings included maps, which could be

Fig. 93

The Politician. Line engraving. May 2, 1771. In this and several other prints maps are shown hung on the walls suspended between wooden rollers. Adapting this practice to the present day, many of the reproduction maps in the buildings are mounted on modern rollers based on an original example in the collection. 1939-234.

either framed or more commonly attached to wood rollers and then hung (fig. 93). Maps seemed to have been hung most often in the public spaces of a house such as the parlor, dining room, or passage and also in the study, but rarely in the bedchamber. Maps also hung in tavern public rooms.

Both decorative and functional, looking glasses also adorned the wall. They were called pier glasses when hung on the wall in the space between two windows or chimney glasses when they were hung above the chimney (fig. 94). After dark, glasses reflected the light emanating from near-by candles. Some looking glasses had attached sconces to hold candles, thereby ensuring maximum reflection of this limited light source (fig. 95). The looking glasses in the public spaces of houses and taverns were often more decorative and expensive than the smaller or simpler versions kept in the more private spaces like the bedchamber.

Despite the features common to all houses, a variety of decorating options meant that each well-to-do eighteenth-century homeowner could create a house suited to his taste. Once decorated, though, these houses did not remain static. By mid-century in Virginia the consumer revolution was influencing the buying habits of the colonists. This resulted in the

Fig. 94

Wetherburn's Tavern Great Room. The inventory for this room listed "1 Large Chimney Do [Glass] £10." To fulfill this requirement we installed a period English example of about 1730-1780 with swinging arms for candles. Surrounding the glass are several horse prints that evoke the interest Virginians had in horses. The top portion of the marble mantel is original to the site while the two vertical side pieces were replicated to complete the fireplace surround.

gentry being able to fill their houses with pieces which earlier in the century might have been beyond their reach.[39] Like today, the owner might chose to rearrange his furnishings or to replace worn-out pieces with newer, more fashionable items. Also, family members came and went requiring nurseries, schoolrooms, or guest chambers. Two hundred years later the same desire to create a convenient and attractive setting in which to live still guides the twentieth-century homeowner.

Fig. 95

A Family Group by Gawen Hamilton. Oil on canvas. England, ca. 1730. The bottom portion of the chimney glass over the fireplace is very similar to the one in the tavern. Since it is still daylight, candles have not yet been placed in the arms. In the eighteenth century candles and candlesticks not in use were stored away until they were required in the evening. 1936-686.

Fig. 96

Capitol Committee Room. Many of the wealthy gentlemen in town were members of the House of Burgesses, which meant that at various times throughout the year they gathered at the Capitol to carry out the government's business. In the room pictured here prominent Virginians met in small groups to discuss and create legislation.

The Town:
To Work and Serve

The furnishing options detailed in the preceding chapters apply to the public and private spaces in the exhibition houses in Williamsburg. Many of these dwellings belonged to the wealthier gentlemen in town who held important positions in government, and some were owners of large estates outside the city as well. Many other people of lesser means resided in the capital city and provided the necessary furnishings, foods, services, and objects with which the gentlemen filled their houses and entertained their guests.

Men like Peyton Randolph and George Wythe, who were involved in government and intellectual pursuits, worked at the Capitol, college, or courthouse as well as continuing to do business at home in their studies (fig. 96). Other men in town also worked at "home," but not in the same way as the gentlemen. Henry Wetherburn, for example, lived with his family in two rooms in the back of the tavern of which he was the owner and innkeeper. These rooms contained furnishings similar to those in the houses of the gentlemen, yet they tended to be less expensive[40] (fig. 97).

James Geddy, the son of the gunsmith James Geddy, was a silversmith in town who lived on the corner of Palace green where he also had his foundry and shop (fig. 98). His shop, the public space from which he sold his goods, is connected to the house while the foundry, the work space wherein the goods were manufactured, is a separate building on the same lot. It was common for the houses of many tradesmen to incorporate not only the living space but the working and selling spaces as well. Many tradesmen in Williamsburg, unable to make a living solely from items of

Fig. 97

Wetherburn's Tavern West Chamber. This room was one of two in the tavern that belonged exclusively to the family. Here Henry Wetherburn kept track of his business dealings while still being able to keep watch over the operation of the tavern. The other room, of about the same size, was a bedchamber for the family.

Fig. 98

James Geddy Foundry. Geddy employed workers to help him produce silver items. This shop is still a working production center as well as a space where visitors can view the eighteenth-century method of creating metal objects. Through the door in the back one can see that the house and shop are just a few steps away.

their own production, supplemented their work with goods imported from England (fig. 99). In a city the size of London it was possible to specialize because of the number of potential customers, but in a town like Williamsburg, the tradesmen found they were more successful when selling a variety of items.

James Anderson, a blacksmith and state armorer during the Revolution, built his forge on the land behind his house. Using eighteenth-century techniques, the Colonial Williamsburg housewrights reconstructed this building in 1985 on the original site (fig. 100). Architectural research based the forge on other Virginia service buildings still extant. Archaeological evidence indicated that the building, which was enlarged several times as Anderson became more successful, held seven forges (fig. 101). Present-day smiths use the forges to demonstrate a variety of

Fig. 99

Man and Child Drinking Tea. Artist unknown. Oil on canvas. England, 1720-1740. In the foreground are portrayed many silver objects of the kind that Geddy might have produced and/or sold. Silver, made into decorative and functional objects, was one way of displaying one's wealth. This unknown sitter has chosen to include these important items in his portrait. 1954-254.

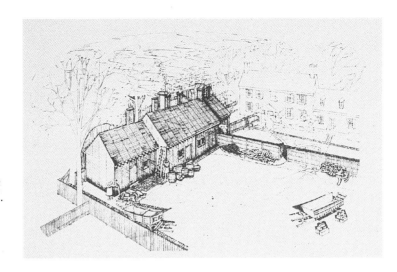

Fig. 100

James Anderson Forge Exterior. Like the Geddy complex, the Anderson Forge stands behind the main house where the family lived. Despite its location the forge does not have a finished look. The building was constructed not for show but for work.

Fig. 101

James Anderson Forge. The interior of the forge shows the extent of the activity carried out in this space. Many smiths as well as their helpers could produce iron objects such as nails, tools, etc. used in other trades in town.

Fig. 102

Fig. 102

Anthony Hay Cabinetmaking
Shop. Gentlemen needed a place to
buy the furniture with which they
furnished their houses. Although
furniture was ordered from agents
in London, many pieces were purchased from local cabinetmakers.
Today the ware room displays furnishings made by the cabinetmakers of Colonial Williamsburg based
on surviving eighteenth-century
Virginia pieces.

blacksmithing techniques while at the same time producing nails, hinges,
tools, and so on that can be used on or in the buildings. The Anthony
Hay Cabinetmaking Shop, an example of another trade, combines the
public sales area with a more private work space. In the eighteenth
century a customer wishing to consult with the cabinetmaker concerning
furnishings for his house entered directly into the ware room of the shop.
In this front room, surrounded by ready-made items displayed for sale, the
customer and cabinetmaker could discuss the possible commission
(fig. 102). A door in this room led to the back of the shop where the
actual manufacturing took place (fig. 103). Like today, the customer did
not necessarily see this side of the business. When Anthony Hay changed

Fig. 103

John Cuff and an Assistant by Johann Zoffany. Oil on canvas. England, 1772. The portrait is unusual in that it portrays a skilled tradesman (here a lens maker) in his working clothes with the shop interior as background, a contrast to the many gentry portraits of the time. Although a specialized shop, it shows the general layout of a workshop and how tools were stored. This information can be used to create shop interiors like the workroom at the Hay shop. Courtesy, Her Majesty the Queen.

Fig. 104

The Patent Wigg. Hand-colored line engraving. England, 1793. This print shows the interior of a barber shop with wigs displayed in the window. The eighteenth-century barber not only cut hair but also worked with wigs since they were worn by most gentlemen. 1956-293.

careers to become the owner and keeper of the Raleigh Tavern, he, as did Wetherburn, lived with his family in rooms at the Raleigh Tavern located up the street from the shop.[41]

These present-day trade shops in Colonial Williamsburg differ from the exhibition buildings already discussed. The tradesmen and interpreters move amid the tools of their trade, raw materials, and finished and unfinished products displayed in the shops (figs. 104 and 105). As more is understood about the trade and use of the tools, the shops can take on a more convincing and realistic look since the work is done on site. The shop interiors are made to look more authentic by not displaying objects where they would be impractical for the workmen or by not cleaning up areas that were obviously meant to be otherwise.

While tradesmen provided furnishings for the houses, another group of townspeople, the slaves, provided the services that maintained the gentry life-style. The domestic dependencies or outbuildings found behind many of the houses were the living and working spaces of the slaves who made up half of the population of eighteenth-century Williamsburg. The support buildings for a house generally consisted of the kitchen, dairy, laundry, stable, smokehouse, well, and privy (fig. 106). These areas were some of the busiest in town with slaves working at daily tasks that ranged from caring for animals to cooking the meals to cleaning the clothes.

The kitchen, the main building in this group of outbuildings, housed the cooking activities that were generally carried out by a slave cook under the supervision of the mistress of the house. Little is known about the slaves on the Wythe property until the 1780s. Lydia was a valued servant who was quite possibly the cook. She could have slept either in the room on the other side of the kitchen fireplace or perhaps upstairs[42] (fig. 107). Many kitchens consisted of a first floor and a half-story above where slaves often slept. Rooms occupied by slaves were also

Fig. 105

The Wigmaker's Shop. The window in which the wigs are displayed is similar to that pictured in figure 104. In the shop the Historic Trades interpreters make wigs from real hair in the eighteenth-century manner for use by some of the character interpreters in town. The tradespeople study not only prints for styles of wigs but also actual surviving wigs to determine their construction.

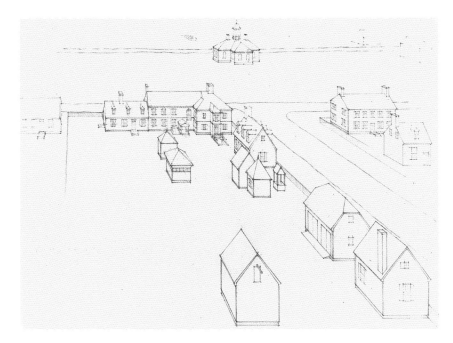

Fig. 106

Architectural Drawing of the Peyton Randolph Yard. Recent archaeological excavations of the backyard of the Peyton Randolph House provided evidence for this conjectural drawing of the outbuildings on this site. Someone of Randolph's social position needed, and could afford, the 27 slaves who worked in this space that had storage, working, and living accommodations.

Fig. 107

George Wythe Kitchen Lydia's Room. Compare this with some of the bedchambers in chapter 3. The furnishings are cheap, simple, and often secondhand. Yet this room was one of the most desirable spaces for a slave because it allowed for some privacy. In the winter heat was provided from the room's fireplace, a luxury many of the slaves did without.

present in the laundry building often located next to the kitchen (fig. 108). Men, women, and children gathered in these areas at the end of a day to eat their meal and enjoy some modicum of family life. Since these spaces were their "house" as well as their work space, slaves also kept their few personal belongings here.

The kitchen is not only a place in which to interpret slave life, but it is in itself another space within the gentry household. Like the other rooms in the house, we use inventories and prints to learn more about its appearance. In looking at kitchen inventories it becomes apparent that kitchens had little movable furniture. However, they were equipped with many objects such as pewter plates, copper pans, iron utensils, earthenware pans, and many other pieces that required storage. Most likely these items were stored on dressers or shelves built into the walls. The dresser was a long table placed against a wall on which foods could be prepared or "dressed." Period British cookbooks refer to work performed on a dresser. They also picture, usually on the frontispiece of these books, an engraving of a kitchen showing this feature[43] (fig. 109). Cooks in Virginia copied these cookery practices as described in the books, although modified to suit the colonial environment.

Like the shops in town, the kitchens are today becoming less static spaces and more work spaces. As present-day cooks work with eighteenth-century equipment and receipts, the period term for recipes, the kitchen begins to take on a more realistic look and feel as the heat from the fire and the smells of the food fill the room (fig. 110). The utensils are placed where they are most needed, and the ones not used are stored as they might have been in the eighteenth century. In order to furnish the kitchens with the appropriate items, studies of many inventories have been combined to create a representative kitchen for a given place and

Fig. 109

Frontispiece to The British Housewife *by Martha Bradley. London, ca. 1770. Pictured on the right is a dresser on which foods could be prepared. Surrounding the door hang shelves that hold the various plates and other kitchen items. While this English kitchen is larger than those in the colonies, the basic items needed in the kitchen remain the same.*

Fig. 110

George Wythe Kitchen. Several times a week the foodways specialists use this kitchen to cook foods with reproduction eighteenth-century utensils. In the eighteenth century this work was most often carried out by slaves under the supervision of the housewife. When the food was ready, it was carried from the kitchen to the dining room.

Fig. 111

Governor's Palace Kitchen. This kitchen, with rooms for storage as well as for cooking, is larger than the one at the Wythe House because larger and more elaborate meals were often called for to entertain the governor's guests. The governor owned a wide range of items that included many copper pots, pans, and molds to aid the preparation of impressive dishes. The workers in this space were a combination of black slaves, white indentured servants, and hired servants who came with the governor from England.

status. For instance, the kitchen of Governor Botetourt contains more elaborate and specialized equipment than that at the Wythe House (fig. 111). Many tavern kitchens would contain larger and more varied utensils than the domestic sites.

The interiors of shops and outbuildings are less well documented in graphic sources than are the interiors of the houses of the gentry. Through written sources, architectural studies, and actual re-creation of the work, an idea of the appearance of such sites can be gained. Many of the trades such as cabinetmaking, silversmithing, and cooking survive today in modified form; through research and experiments, they can be recaptured to present a plausible and animated reconstruction of the past.

Conclusion

Since Colonial Williamsburg opened the Raleigh Tavern as its first exhibition building in 1932, the number of historic buildings opened to visitors has grown, accompanied by an increase in knowledge about the eighteenth-century town. The work leading up to these openings was possible due to the continuous research efforts of many departments. The search for information about any site or subject is never completed. New sources and areas of study continually reveal further aspects of colonial life that may change the ideas we previously held. The buildings and interpretation change to reflect this knowledge. Even the most recent photography may soon become obsolete when new information, previously unknown or misunderstood, is evaluated and used to update the furnishing plan.

While the documents and paintings can show us generally what the interior of a house was like, each house remains unique. Each owner had the opportunity to furnish his house the way he liked according to his own taste and means. Despite the standard furnishings of beds, a few chairs, and a dressing table, every bedchamber could look remarkably different by changing the textiles on the bed and chairs, covering the table, or installing simple, inexpensive furniture rather than that of the latest fashion. As we learn more about the owner of the house, we are better able to judge what his choices might have been. Once furnished, the buildings serve not only to showcase the vast collection of colonial and English furniture, ceramics, textiles, silver, and more but also to provide visitors with a way of comprehending the life and habits of the occupants of two hundred years ago.

Since the buildings are used as a visual means of presenting the visitor with an understanding of the people and life-styles of the past, it is important that each room is as complete a picture as possible. While sources such as inventories give the number of pieces to be placed in a room, it is not always possible to display the correct amount using the museum's present collection of antiques. In some cases an appropriate antique exists but because of its condition cannot safely be put on exhibit. In such circumstances a reproduction is made of that antique which is as appropriate as we can come to the time, social and economic level, and personal circumstances we are striving to depict. Such furnishings can be used, not to masquerade as an antique, but to help complete the setting. For instance, the Peyton Randolph inventory calls for a set of twelve chairs. One chair in the collection had a history of having been made in

Williamsburg and descended in a Williamsburg family. This was a perfect chair for the space, but only one of the original set had been given to the Foundation. Therefore the cabinetmakers at the Anthony Hay Shop reproduced the chair, making twelve of them which are now on display at the Peyton Randolph House. With all the pieces in place the visitor more fully understands the use and users of the rooms and objects.

Colonial Williamsburg offers two ways to study the material world of the past. At the DeWitt Wallace Decorative Arts Gallery a visitor can view the objects closely in a traditional museum setting and compare them with similar pieces. There one can delight in the beauty and quality of the object. In the buildings the visitor is able to view the objects in their eighteenth-century context as they were meant to be seen. Encountering the furnishings in place reminds the visitor that the original owners sat on, ate off of, and slept upon these objects. With the opportunity to view the material goods of the eighteenth century in these two ways, a visitor can more fully appreciate the furnishings as objects of art as well as household items used by the original owners.

While there are differences between the houses of the past and those of today, there are also similarities. Many of the room divisions and usages found in modern homes were just emerging in the colonial period. Houses of today also have dining rooms, parlors, bedchambers, and studies. While the rooms might be called by different names, they are nonetheless familiar and recognizable. Twentieth-century homeowners entertain, eat, read, and sleep in their houses just as George and Elizabeth Wythe, Peyton and Betty Randolph, and Thomas Everard did in theirs. Through the careful re-creation of their eighteenth-century interiors, visitors encounter a setting in which to understand, appreciate, and enjoy the life of eighteenth-century Virginians.

Notes

[1] Out of 47 room-by-room inventories examined for eastern Virginia between 1750 and 1800, 35 still had halls and only 11, primarily well-to-do individuals, had parlors. For a fuller discussion of the development of the passage, dining room, and parlor, see Mark R. Wenger, "The Central Passage in Virginia: Evolution of an Eighteenth-Century Living Space," in *Perspectives in Vernacular Architecture*, II, ed. Camille Wells (Columbia, Mo., 1986), pp. 137–149; and Mark R. Wenger, "The Dining Room in Early Virginia," in *Perspectives in Vernacular Architecture*, III, ed. Thomas Carter and Bernard L. Herman (Columbia, Mo., 1989), pp. 149–159. For a discussion of these architectural spaces in less academic or gentry settings, see Dell Upton, "Vernacular Domestic Architecture in Eighteenth-Century Virginia," *Winterthur Portfolio*, XVII (1982), pp. 95–119.

[2] "The Governor's Palace: An Inventory of the Personal Estate of His Excellency Lord Botetourt Began to be Taken the 24th of Octo‍ʳ 1770," in *Inventories of Four Eighteenth-Century Houses in the Historic Area of Williamsburg* [Williamsburg, Va., 1974], p. 9.

[3] Appraisement of the Estate of William Hunter Esquire deceased 24th August 1761, York County, Virginia, Records, Wills and Inventories, XXI, 1760–1774, pp. 79–82, microfilm, Colonial Williamsburg Foundation.

[4] Hugh Jones, *The Present State of Virginia*, ed. Richard L. Morton (Chapel Hill, N. C., 1956), p. 71, as quoted in Wenger, "Central Passage," p. 139. See also *ibid.*, p. 148; Edward Miles Riley, ed., *The Journal of John Harrower: An Indentured Servant in the Colony of Virginia, 1773–1776* (Williamsburg, Va., 1963), p. 104; and Jack P. Greene, ed., *The Diary of Colonel Landon Carter of Sabine Hall, 1752–1778*, II (Charlottesville, Va., 1965), p. 944.

[5] Mark Girouard, *Life in an English Country House: A Social and Architectural History* (New Haven, Conn., 1978), p. 203. See also *ibid.*, pp. 104, 162.

[6] Wenger, "Dining Room in Early Virginia," p. 154. This analysis is derived from Wenger's article as well as from Upton, "Vernacular Domestic Architecture," pp. 95–119.

[7] Willie Graham, "Building an Image: An Architectural Report on the Peyton Randolph Site," pp. 8, 11–12, research report, 1985, CWF.

[8] "Peyton Randolph House: Inventory and Appraisement of the Estate of Peyton Randolph Esqr. in York County Taken Janr. the 5th. 1776," in *Inventories of Four Eighteenth-Century Houses*, p. 24.

[9] Hunter Dickinson Farish, ed., *The Journal & Letters of Philip Vickers Fithian, 1773–1774: A Plantation Tutor of the Old Dominion* (Williamsburg, Va., 1957), p. 95.

[10] *Ibid.*, p. 80.

[11] "Governor's Palace Inventory," p. 11. The inventory entry calls for "3 blue Moreen Window Curtains belonging to the dining Room." These curtains were stored in an upstairs closet.

[12] "Peyton Randolph Inventory," p. 24; "Governor's Palace Inventory," pp. 10, 15. Most of the cloths are listed under a separate category of linens. The governor had a total of 53 dinner cloths of varying sizes and 57 breakfast cloths. Accompanying the dinner cloths were 32 1/2 dozen napkins. Each cloth had a specific set of napkins listed in conjunction with it.

[13] In 1769 George Washington "dined with the Council and spent the Evening in the Daphne" where he may have eaten, drunk, or played cards with other gentlemen. Donald Jackson, ed., *The Diaries of George Washington*. II: *1766–1770* (Charlottesville, Va., 1976), p. 148.

[14] Girouard, *Life in the English Country House*, p. 99.

[15] One Virginian ordered from London "One smaller peice of blue grounded Cotton of the same sort [as the bed] for Window Curtains with binding and Rings for the whole." Frances Norton Mason, ed., *John Norton & Sons, Merchants of London and Virginia* (Richmond, Va., 1937), p. 190.

[16] Riley, ed., *Journal of Harrower*, p. 57.

[17] While traveling in the colonies Fithian described his accommodations: "I slept in a Room with seven of them, and one for a Bedfellow; he was however clean, and civel, and our Beds were good and neat." Robert Albion Greenhalgh and Leonidas Dodson, eds., *Philip Vickers Fithian: Journal, 1775–1776, Written on the Virginia-Pennsylvania Frontier and in the Army around New York* (Princeton, N. J., 1934), p. 39.

[18] "Wetherburn's Tavern: The Inventory and Appraisement of the Estate of Henry Wetherburn in York County," in *Inventories of Four Eighteenth-Century Houses*, pp. 27–29; "Peyton Randolph House Inventory," pp. 25–26.

[19] "Raleigh Tavern: Inventory and Appraisement of the Estate of Anthony Hay late of the City of Williamsburg Tavern Keeper Deceased," in *Inventories of Four Eighteenth-Century Houses*, p. 20. Among the furnishings for the rooms upstairs are "3 White Window Curtains."

[20] Girouard, *Life in the English Country House*, p. 166. See *ibid.*, pp. 165–170, for a discussion of the library's evolution in England.

[21] Richard Beale Davis, *Intellectual Life in the Colonial South 1585–1763*, II (Knoxville, Tenn., 1978), p. 501.

[22] Inventory of Major Peter Walker, Northampton Co., Virginia, Records, Orders, VI, 1655/6, pp. 109–111, microfilm, CWF.

[23] Accomack Co., Virginia, Records, Wills Etc. Orders, 1682–1697, pp. 213–216, typescript, CWF.

[24] Samuel Johnson, *A Dictionary of the English Language* (1755; reprint, New York, 1979).

[25] Mark R. Wenger to Travis C. McDonald, May 28, 1987, CWF.

[26] Littleton Waller Tazewell, "An Account and History of the Tazewell Family," quoted in Mary R. M. Goodwin, "The George Wythe House: Its Furniture and Furnishings," p. 10, research report, 1958, CWF.

[27] "Governor's Palace Inventory," pp. 8, 18. For a list of books, see *ibid.*, pp. 16–17.

[28] "Peyton Randolph House Inventory," p. 25.

[29] Susanna Whatman, *The Housekeeping Book of Susanna Whatman 1776–1800*, introduction by Christina Hardyment (1956; reprint, London, 1987), pp. 38–39.

[30] A study of Williamsburg inventories reveals that window curtains, while not standard furnishings, occurred in quite a few houses throughout the century. They most frequently appear in the bedchambers and were relatively inexpensive especially compared to the prices of the other textiles in the room.

[31] Whatman, *Housekeeping Book*, p. 21. See also Hannah Glasse, *The Servants Directory, or, House-keeper's Companion* (London, 1760), pp. 29–31.

[32] Mason, ed., *Norton & Sons*, p. 348.

[33] Purdie and Dixon's *Virginia Gazette* (Williamsburg), Dec. 28, 1769.

[34] "Governor's Palace Inventory," p. 5.

[35] One observer in Virginia noted "good carpeting tends to concentrate the heat, which is an advantage in a country where . . . rooms are drafty." Kenneth Roberts and Anna M. Roberts, trans. and eds., *Moreau de St. Mery's American Journey* (Garden City, N. Y., 1947), p. 326.

[36] Burning fires had to be tended carefully. Col. James Gordon noted a time in Feb. 1759 when "a coal of fire rolled on the dining-room floor and burned a great hole in the plank." Susanna Whatman warned that "no carpet in any of the rooms should be laid nearer than the wooden edge of the hearth." "The Journal of Col. James Gordon, of Lancaster County, Va.," *William and Mary Quarterly*, 1st Ser., XI (1902), p. 101; Whatman, *Housekeeping Book*, p. 42.

[37] "Governor's Palace Inventory," pp. 5–6, 11. As part of the seasonal changes made in the historic buildings, the fireplace tools had been taken out and stored during the summer. Recent research though has shown that this might not have been the practice in some houses in eighteenth-century Virginia. Susanne Olson, "Fireplace Equipment and Keeping Fires During the Summer Months," research report, 1989, CWF.

[38] Robert Beverley to Samuel Athawes, Apr. 15, 1771, Robert Beverley Letter Book, 1761–1793, Beverley Papers, Library of Congress, transcript, CWF.

[39] For a detailed discussion of the consumer revolution, see Neil McKendrick, John Brewer, and J. H. Plumb, *The Birth of a Consumer Society: The Commercialization of Eighteenth-Century England* (Bloomington, Ind., 1982); and Carole Shammas, *The Pre-Industrial Consumer in England and America* (Oxford, 1990). For its effects on the colonies, see Jack P. Greene and J. R. Pole, eds., *Colonial British America: Essays in the New History of the Early Modern Era* (Baltimore, 1984), particularly the essay by Richard L. Bushman, "American High-Style and Vernacular Cultures," pp. 345–383.

[40] "Wetherburn's Tavern Inventory," p. 27. The entries listed under the heading "In the Chamber" apply to both of the back rooms set aside for the family.

[41] A letter from Sarah Trebell to her brother John Galt written in Jan. 1767 recently was acquired by Colonial Williamsburg. This one letter gave us new evidence that the Hay family lived at the tavern. Sarah Trebell wrote, "Mr Trebell has sold the Raliegh to A. Hay who now lives there and all his little family." With this knowledge, some of the entries in the inventory of the Raleigh Tavern made more sense in that there are listings of furnishings for rooms which were more appropriate for a private space than a tavern. Transcript by Ronald Hurst, 1989, CWF.

[42] The information about Wythe's slaves comes from the personal property tax lists made in the 1780s. Lydia is not specifically designated as the cook, but the cook Lydia Broadnax was working for Wythe at the beginning of the nineteenth century. These two Lydias are quite possibly the same person. Wythe freed Lydia in 1787, but she remained with the family. Cathleene Hellier to Ronald Hurst, May 4, 1987, CWF.

[43] Donna C. Hole, "The Kitchen Dresser: Architectural Fittings in Eighteenth and Early Nineteenth Century Anglo-American Kitchens," *Petits Propos Culinaires*, IX (October 1981), pp. 25–33.

Glossary

ANDIRONS (endirons, doggs, hand irons, fire doggs). Objects made of iron or other metal used in the fireplace or hearth on which the wood rests while burning. They have a horizontal bar raised slightly above the ground with a vertical piece (often made of brass) at the front that is usually ornamental but also holds the wood in place. Andirons often appear in inventories in connection with other fireplace tools—tongs, poker, and shovel.

ASSEMBLY. In 1751 an assembly was defined as "a stated and general meeting of the polite persons of both sexes, for the sake of conversation, gallantry, news, and play." This gathering, often held at a tavern or other public building, generally took place in the evening. A ticket purchased for the event covered the cost of admittance and food (if any).

BALL. Dr. Samuel Johnson defined a ball as "an entertainment of dancing, at which the preparations are made at the expence of some particular person," as opposed to an assembly which was a public gathering paid for by subscription. The governor held balls at the Palace that included dancing in the ballroom and an elegant supper in the supper room.

BED. In the eighteenth century this term was used most often to refer to the tick stuffed with feathers which was then raised above the floor on a bedstead. Less frequently it could refer to the entire assemblage of bedding, much as we use it today. In Dr. Johnson's dictionary "bed" is defined as "something made to sleep on." In period inventories the bed is often listed as one of a group of bedding that consisted of pillow, bolster, curtains, etc.

BED ROUND. A floor covering pieced together to form a "U" shape which, when placed around the bed, gives the appearance of a full carpet (especially in cases where the base valances concealed the area under the bed). Because carpeting was expensive, this solution was economical as well as attractive.

BEDSTEAD. A wooden frame, either high or low post, upon which the bed or mattress was placed. Owing to construction of the frame, which was held together by screws, it could be assembled or disassembled easily. Cheaper rope bedsteads supported the bed on a network of ropes that were threaded through holes in the rails and tightened to support the weight of the sleeper and

bedding. More expensive bedsteads had pins on the bed rails to receive a linen sacking bottom also designed for support.

BLIND (VENETIAN). A type of window shade made of wooden laths held together by tapes and connected to a series of pulleys so that they could be raised and lowered as desired. The laths were positioned to permit the passage of air without allowing much harmful light. Today in exhibit spaces venetian blinds provide protection from sunlight while still maintaining the integrity of the period interior.

BLUE AND WHITE. China. Judging by the quantities of wares excavated in the tidewater area, the majority of blue and white "China" listed in inventories was probably Chinese export hard-paste porcelain. Blue and white soft-paste porcelain was being produced in lesser quantities in England. By the latter part of the eighteenth century the term blue and white might refer to some pearlware, a lead-glazed earthenware.

BOLSTER (boulster). A long pillow filled with a firm material that extended across the head of the bed. Some beds were equipped with only the bolster in which case it was stuffed with a soft material such as feathers. A firm bolster was used in conjunction with softer, smaller pillows. The bolster prevented the additional pillows from slipping down between the headboard and the bed.

BOWFAT (buffet, beaufat, beauffet, bofett). A closet or cupboard (often built into the wall) where ceramics, glass, and/or silver could be displayed as well as stored while not in use. Johnson noted in his definition that shelves for display were often found "in a room of entertainment."

CAMP BED (see FIELD BED).

CANDLESTICK. A stand made of brass, silver, iron, tin, glass, or ceramic that holds a candle.

CARPET. Johnson defined a carpet as "A covering of various colours, spread upon floors or tables." By the middle of the eighteenth century carpets were almost exclusively used on the floor, as opposed to "ruggs," which were heavy bed covers.

CHAFING DISH (chafin). A portable grate that held burning coals and could be set on a metal stand. It provided a way of transporting hot coals to other fires or to set on the table to be used to light gentlemen's pipes.

CHAMBER. This term most often referred to the room designated as the sleeping area or to a room that was appropriated for use by one or two people. Not as commonly used to refer to the public rooms of the house.

CHAMBERSTICK. The stand holding a candle that is most often used next to the bed. A chamberstick is shorter than a regular candlestick and has a small handle on the side so that it can easily be carried to light the way to the bedchamber at night. The base of the chamberstick is a wide, shallow bowl to prevent melting wax from falling on the floor, carpet, or clothing. Also called a "flat" or "hand" candlestick.

CHANDELIER. A lighting device suspended from the ceiling. It usually consisted of several arms, also called branches, each of which held a candle. It could be made of brass, glass, wood, etc. Rarely used in domestic interiors in Virginia; more often found in public rooms.

CHEST of DRAWERS. A piece of furniture made up of a series of drawers used for storing clothing or other articles.

CHIMNEY BOARD. Made of a piece of wood or of wallpaper and canvas stretched on a wooden frame, it was used to cover the fireplace opening in summer. It could be painted a single color or with a scene.

CHIMNEY GLASS. A looking glass made to be hung horizontally over the fireplace.

CHINA. Referred primarily to porcelains, whether of English or Chinese origin, and, to a lesser degree, to finer earthenwares.

CLOAK PIN. A brass knob that was attached to a bed post around which the cords from the bed curtains could be secured, thus allowing the curtains to drape and hang open. Cloak pins were decorative as well as functional elements. They might also be used at windows to secure the cords of the window curtains.

CLOSE STOOL. A chair adapted or made specifically to accommodate a chamber pot beneath its seat.

CLOSET. Johnson defined this space as "a small room of privacy and retirement" and as "a private repository of curiosities and valuable things." In some houses it was used as storage for a library of books. Although some closets were located off the bedchamber, they were not as commonly used for clothing storage as they are today.

COUCH. According to Johnson, "a seat of repose, on which it is common to lye down dressed." Usually this piece has an "arm" on only one side and, occasionally, a half-back.

COUNTERPANE (counterpin, counterpain, counterpayne). A woven covering for the bed, most often ornamental.

COVERLET (coverlids). Johnson defined this as "the outermost of the bedcloaths; that under which all the rest are concealed."

CURTAIN. A cloth that can be pulled together or left open to admit the desired amount of light. It can refer to the hangings of either a bed or a window. Some bedchambers in the eighteenth century included both window and bed curtains. When looking at inventories, caution must be used in determining the type of curtains to which the entry refers.

DAMASK. A fabric woven in a pattern, made reversible, and generally in a single color. It could be composed of either a single fiber such as silk or a combination of fibers such as worsted and silk. Depending on its material, damask was an expensive and elegant fabric.

DELFT (delph, delf). Dutch earthenware with a tin-enamel glaze, a white body with blue decoration. In the seventeenth century the English created an earthenware to imitate this Dutch ceramic from the city of Delft. By the eighteenth century "delph," as it appears in inventories, referred to this English version. The addition of tin to the lead glaze produced an opaque white ground well suited to colored decoration. Johnson defined "delf" as "counterfeit China ware" since many of the designs were patterned after Chinese examples.

DESK. A box or table with a sloping front on which to write. This could refer to a portable writing desk that a gentleman could carry with him when he traveled or to a case piece with drawers and a surface for writing. One way to determine which type of desk is mentioned in an inventory is to look at the value of the piece. "Desk" when used in conjunction with "bookcase" referred to the lower portion of a case piece that had drawers as well as a sloping front that opened to reveal a writing surface and a place to store papers.

DINING ROOM. By the last quarter of the eighteenth century Johnson defined this space as "the principal apartment of the house; the room where entertainments are made." In this period the dinner meal had become a formal and elegant affair to which guests were often invited.

The room in which dinner was served was furnished with dining tables and matched sets of chairs. Also in this space a gentleman displayed his wealth and taste through the presence of ceramics and silver.

DINNER. The main meal of the day served about two or three o'clock in the afternoon. In Virginia dinner usually comprised two courses. The first consisted of meats and vegetables, and the second of dessert items such as pies, puddings, and tarts.

DINNER SERVICE. As dining became an important ritual to the gentry, the dining equipment that accompanied the service of the food increased. Matched sets of china became more prevalent and consisted of a variety of sizes and shapes from standard round dinner plates (about 9 to 10 inches in diameter) to bowls to larger serving pieces either round or oval. Flatware too came in sets usually of a dozen or more. These sets included knives and forks, while tablespoons were often purchased as their own set since they were usually made entirely of silver rather than having handles of another material as the knives and forks tended to have.

DRESSING GLASS. A looking glass having an easel back or connected to a wooden stand that was of a size appropriate for the top of a dressing table. The stand might have a drawer for storage of toilet articles or valuables. The glass could be adjusted in the frame for more effective use. Also a small framed glass without a stand that hung on the wall in a bedchamber.

EARTHEN (earthen ware). Ceramics less valuable than the finer porcelains and queensware. Rough red earthenwares would fit into this group, as would tortoiseshell or black-glazed pieces and other colored glazed pieces.

EASY CHAIR (easie chair). An upholstered chair with arms and side pieces (wings) that was most often kept in the bedchamber. The sitter would be protected from drafts by the side elements, which also served to catch and hold the heat from the fire when the chair was properly positioned.

ELBOW CHAIR. A common inventory entry referring to a chair with arms.

ENAMEL (enamd). The method of decorating ceramics by applying colors over the glaze of the piece in firings subsequent to burning the body and fixing the glaze. Although colors could also be applied under or "in" the glaze, the value of the piece increased with added firings because of the danger of breakage that occurred with each firing.

EN SUITE. A French term used to denote that a group of objects have a common element and belong together. Most often used to refer to the textiles in a room when they are all of the same fabric.

ENTERTAINMENT. Johnson gave three related definitions for this term: "1. Conversation; 2. Treatment at the table; convivial provision; 3. Hospitable reception."

ENTRY. The space into which one enters the house from the outside. The term is found in some inventories and can refer to the passage.

EPERGNE. A large silver or ceramic piece used as a centerpiece for a table. It consisted of a center vessel with arms extending outward that might support smaller containers. The whole was filled with flowers, fruits, sweetmeats, nuts, etc.

ESCRITOIRE (scritore, scrutore, screwtore, escrutore). A case piece of furniture now referred to as a secretary or bureau. It consisted of a top section with doors that concealed shelves for storage of books or papers and a bottom portion consisting of a series of drawers. Similar to a desk and bookcase.

FENDER. A metal piece extending the length of the fireplace and a few inches high that is set before a fire to prevent falling coals from rolling forward onto the floor.

FIELD BED. A portable bed frame that was easily transported by those moving about in the field. Like other bedsteads, this could be high or low post, and in the case of the former would have a set of bed curtains. The tester of such a high-post bed was often curvilinear and had an additional piece of fabric to enclose the top. In domestic inventories "field bed" most commonly refers to a non-folding bedstead that was similar in shape to a military folding bedstead. These domestic examples were rarely low post, always curtained.

FIRE DOGS (see ANDIRONS).

FLOOR CLOTH (oyl cloth, passage cloth). A floor covering made of canvas painted and oiled several times to create a hard, durable surface that was also washable. Most often used in areas with high traffic where an expensive carpet was vulnerable to wear.

FURNITURE. Johnson gave three definitions for this word: "1. Moveables, goods put in a house for use or ornament. 2. Appendages. 3. Equipage; embellishments; decorations." In the eighteenth century furniture, as in the phrase "bed furniture," referred to the hangings, coverings, etc. that made up the bed.

GARNITURE. Defined by Johnson as "furniture; ornament." It refers to the small objects such as vases or ceramic figures, frequently sold in sets, that were placed on the mantel of a fireplace.

GIRANDOLE. Similar to a sconce. A branched candlestick or a fixed bracket for holding candles. In the mid-eighteenth century this term was often used to refer to branches attached to an open-work frame of carved, gilt wood usually surrounding a looking glass.

GRATE. A metal structure either freestanding or built into the fireplace in which the fire would be made. Although the grates were used with wood fires, they were ideal for coal fires that were becoming more common by the end of the eighteenth century. Although andirons were still common in most houses, grates were found in wealthier households as well as in higher status kitchens.

HALL. A public room in the house generally used for a variety of purposes. At the beginning of the century, this was the largest room in the house and was used for dining, entertaining, and sometimes sleeping. Later in the century, several of these functions were relegated to other rooms in the house, leaving the hall to accommodate the activities between meals.

HEADCLOTH. On a high-post bedstead, a piece of cloth that hangs at the head of the bed suspended from the tester frame or metal rod and in front of the headboard.

IMAGES. Ceramic figures. The subject matter varied from popular heros to legendary, classical, pastoral, or animal subjects.

LANTERN (lanthorn). A lighting device that could be hung from the ceiling or carried by hand. A case often made of glass and metal or wood in the center of which sat the candle where it was protected from drafts and permitted reflection.

LIBRARY. A collection of books usually found in the study, although books were also kept in the hall, bedchamber, and, earlier in the eighteenth century, in closets.

LOOKING GLASS. The period term for a mirror. These were expensive items found in the dining room, parlor, passage, and occasionally in bedchambers.

LUMBER. Johnson defined "lumber" as "any thing useless or cumbersome; any thing of more bulk than value." These items were not often used by the family but were not thrown away either.

Some houses had a lumber room that was equivalent in many ways to a modern attic except that the lumber room was located on the second floor. It was essentially a storage room.

LUSTRE. A category of glass lighting device, including chandeliers, sconces, and other elaborate candle holders, many with prism-like pendants.

MATTRESS. A sack made of canvas or linen and stuffed with hair, straw, or other material on top of which could be laid the bed. The mattress could be used by itself as well.

NIGHT TABLE. A table, found chiefly in bedchambers, enclosing a portable chamber pot or fitted with a pullout seat that suggests the presence of one. The top can be fitted with rails around the side and the whole case mounted on legs.

ORNAMENTAL. China pieces that included a range from purely decorative wares such as figures to limited use wares such as vases or elaborate table pieces.

PALLET. A sack filled with straw or similar material laid directly on the floor. Often seen in reference to slave bedding.

PARLOR (see also HALL). A room in a house commonly used for entertaining guests or as a sitting room for the family. Johnson referred to it as being "elegantly furnished for reception or entertainment." If a house had both a dining room and a parlor, the parlor was generally the room in which guests sat before and after dinner and where they could play cards or take tea. It derives from the room earlier known as the hall.

PASSAGE. The space that usually extends the width of the house. The other rooms of the house are reached through doorways off this space. The passage can refer to either the upstairs or downstairs area. Although this space allowed access to other rooms, it was used as a room itself, especially during warm weather.

PIER. The solid portion of the wall between windows or doors. Used as an adjective to denote furnishings that are placed in this area such as a pier table or a pier glass.

PILLOW. Defined by Johnson as "a bag of down or feathers laid under the head to sleep on." This differs from a bolster in that the pillow is smaller, being about the same size as today's standard pillow.

PLATE. 1. Silver pieces such as candlesticks, tablewares, etc. Johnson defined "plate" as "wrought silver." Often in inventories the amount of plate owned is listed in ounces rather than by the piece.

2. The shallow vessel from which a person eats his meal.

PRESS. A case piece of furniture with shelves designed to hold clothes, books, or ceramics. A clothespress has shelves, some of which slide out for easier access to the folded clothing, that are enclosed with solid doors. A bookpress is usually a taller piece with stationary shelves and solid or glass doors. In the latter instance, a curtain would be hung on the inside of the glass to protect the books from light.

PRESS BED. A bedstead made to fit into a cupboard or press. When the door to the piece was opened, the bed would fold down and could be outfitted with a full complement of bed furniture.

PYRAMID. A table decoration in the shape of a pyramid. Usually "pyramid" referred to two or three footed glass salvers of graduated sizes set one on top of the other. Jelly and syllabub glasses were placed on the salvers. The salvers could be topped with a small salver or with a sweetmeat glass. In diagrams of table settings that appear in eighteenth-century cookbooks, pyramids were often placed in the center of the table during the second course of dinner or during a supper.

QUEEN'S CHINA (Queensware). The most common term used in the Chesapeake area for cream colored earthenware known as creamware in England. This pale, highly refined earthenware body with a lead glaze was perfected in the 1760s in Staffordshire and Yorkshire. The term "Queen's Ware" was coined by Josiah Wedgwood of Staffordshire, who was commissioned to produce a service in this material for Queen Charlotte. Because this china could be manufactured cheaply, it became possible for the middle class to afford complete sets of dinnerware. By the 1770s this china was fashionable in Virginia.

QUILT. A covering for a bed made from at least two pieces of cloth with a soft substance between, and then all stitched together. Another form of quilt, called cord quilting, consisted of two pieces of material sewn together with a cord run between them in a series of designs and sewn in place.

RED AND WHITE. China, known today as "Imari." Somewhat less common than the blue and white Chinese export hard-paste porcelain wares. This type of decoration included much blue patterning but was enhanced with a deep orange red

and sometimes with gilding.

RUG (rugg). In the eighteenth century this word, according to Johnson, referred to "a coarse nappy coverlet used for mean beds." Some of these heavy bed coverings were of needlework, often of varying colors and designs.

SCONCE. A form of candlestick either to be hung directly on the wall or attached to the frame of a looking glass.

SCOTCH CARPET. Known as an ingrain carpet, a non-pile reversible carpet made from colorful, dyed wools before being woven in long, narrow strips. As with other woven carpets, these strips are then sewn together to make larger carpets that were sometimes finished with contrasting borders. The name refers to the fact that they were manufactured primarily in Scotland.

SETTEE. A piece of seating furniture with a back and arms that is made to seat two or more people. Some settees were made as part of a set of side chairs and thus they look as if two or three chairs were fixed together. Other settees are upholstered on both the seat and the back.

SHUTTER. A piece of wood found on either the interior (usually on brick houses) or exterior (usually on frame houses) of the window. A shutter could be made of a solid panel of wood or of immobile slats. Interior shutters were solid and each was made of a single vertical panel or two that were hinged together. When closed to block out the light, shutters could be held shut with a bar across them.

SIDEBOARD (sideboard table). A table made to stand to the side of a room and function as a secondary table on which to set side dishes, beverages, and glasses. Most often found in the dining room. Unlike the main dishes of a meal, beverages did not appear on the table until the guests were already seated and could request a drink, which was dispensed from this side table. This table might also function as the place where one's silver pieces could be displayed during a meal. Not until the 1780s did the sideboard (used without "table") evolve into a case piece with storage for wine bottles, silver, and linens.

SOFA. This upholstered piece is similar in construction to a settee but is made more comfortable for reclining. Although popular in other colonies, it was not commonly found in colonial Virginia houses.

STAFFORDSHIRE. Lead-glazed earthenwares (and possibly porcelains) of various descriptions.

These could include tortoiseshell or black-glazed pieces as well as queensware, pearlware, or other materials. Despite the name, the term does not apply exclusively to ceramics specifically produced in that county of England.

STONE (stoneware). A clay body fired to a temperature between earthenware and porcelain and made impervious with a glaze created when salt reacts with the heat in a kiln. The ware was produced in white or brown and sometimes decorated in colors.

STUDY. A room in the house set aside for reading, business, and other intellectual pursuits. Often such a room was furnished with books, desks, presses, chairs, and, in some cases, scientific apparatus. Such single purpose rooms were unusual in Virginia except in the wealthiest houses.

SUPPER. A light meal served about eight or nine o'clock in the evening. The foods composing this meal generally consisted of a few meats and sweet dishes. For special occasions it might be accompanied by a ball or other entertainment.

TALL CASE CLOCK (long case). Today referred to as a grandfather clock. Developed in the seventeenth century, the long swinging pendulum of the clock allowed it to keep time more accurately. These pieces were usually over six feet tall. They were decorative pieces made in the latest furniture styles as well as practical devices for keeping track of time. Due to their high cost, clocks in Virginia were owned chiefly by the wealthiest people.

TEA. By the middle of the eighteenth century tea had become a popular beverage, the drinking of which was a ritual carried on in many households. Generally tea was served in the afternoon following dinner. Because of its popularity, ceramic services just for tea were made and are often found grouped together in an inventory. Some services are found in the bedchamber, while others appear in the parlor. Tea was generally served in the parlor, although if a group consisted only of ladies or the family, tea could be served in the bedchamber (where tea tables were occasionally kept) or in the passage in summer. The tea service consisted of cups, saucers, teapot, tea kettle, teaspoons, sugar tongs, sugar bowl, slop basin, and a cream or milk jug.

TEA BOARD. A large wooden or metal tray on which a tea service can be carried or stored.

TESTER (teaster). On a high-post bed, a piece of canvas, linen, or material en suite with the rest of the bed textiles stretched on a wooden frame that covered the top of the bedstead between the four posts creating a kind of ceiling for the bedstead. This protected the sleeper from drafts and prevented dust from falling on the bed.

TOILET (toylet, twilight). Johnson defined this simply as "a dressing table." The word refers not only to the piece of furniture but also to the process of preparing oneself with makeup, perfume, etc. It can also refer to the group of objects associated with such a process or to the skirted linen or cotton cover on a dressing table.

TORTOISE. Although natural tortoiseshell was a popular material in the eighteenth century, the term "tortoise" was also used to describe pale lead-glazed earthenware that was decorated, often by sponging, with underglaze colored oxides.

TOW. "Flax or hemp beaten and combed into a filamentous substance," according to Johnson. This material was used for stuffing mattresses on which people slept.

TOY. Defined by Johnson as "a petty commodity; a trifle; a thing of no value." While "toy" could refer to children's playthings, it more often denoted small items such as kitchen tools and personal accessories. In ceramic terms, it referred to figures and other ornamental wares such as keepsake boxes in ceramic or enamel and miniature tea or table wares.

TRUCKLE BED (trundle bed, trunnel, trunkle). A bedstead low to the ground and set on wheels so that it could be pushed under a higher bedstead. This provided extra sleeping space when needed but did not take up extra room in the day. The term "truckle bed" probably derives from "truckle," the casters on which the bedstead rolled.

TURKEY CARPET. The period term for an oriental carpet. The first oriental carpets imported into England seem to have come from Turkey and were especially popular in the seventeenth and eighteenth centuries. Turkey carpets should not be confused with Turkey-work carpets, which were English-made examples in the popular Turkish style.

UPHOLSTERER. In the eighteenth century this term was used to describe "One who furnishes houses; one who fits up apartments with beds and furniture."

VALANCE (vallens). The horizontal piece of fabric suspended from the upper and/or lower rails of the bed. These pieces on the upper frame between the bedposts hid the hardware from which the curtains were hung. A high-post bed with its full complement of furniture would consist of both inner and outer valances as well as base valances. The inner valances around the top hid the hardware from the occupant of the bed. The entire ensemble was of the same fabric. "Valance" can also refer to the piece of fabric hung across the top of a window curtain that served the same purpose as the bed valances.

WAINSCOT (wainscoat, wainscut). Used as both a noun and a verb, it refers to the architectural embellishment and procedure of fitting the wall with panels of wood. Generally these panels extend from the floor to the chair rail (about a third of the way up the wall). This term is also used to describe pieces of furniture made from large boards.

WAITER. An object, usually of wood or metal, that is used to carry objects from one area to the other. The term can refer to trays, salvers, boards, etc. and is usually used in conjunction with dining when glasses, dishes, and other items needed to be moved from the table to the sideboard or to another room.

WILTON CARPET. A floor covering made of worsted fibers in a variety of colors that was very popular in the last thirty years of the eighteenth century. Wilton carpets were constructed the same as Brussels carpets except that the pile of the Brussels was left uncut, giving it a looped surface, while the Wilton was cut, giving it a velvet pile. The name Wilton comes from the town in England that was noted for its carpet manufacturing since the time of Queen Elizabeth I. These carpets were loom woven, as opposed to the hand-knotted Turkey carpets. The pieces were woven in strips and then seamed together to the desired size.

Bibliography

Austin, John C. *Chelsea Porcelain at Williamsburg.* Williamsburg, Va.: Colonial Williamsburg Foundation, 1977.

Carson, Barbara. *The Governor's Palace: The Williamsburg Residence of Virginia's Royal Governor.* Williamsburg, Va.: Colonial Williamsburg Foundation, 1987.

Carson, Cary, Norman F. Barka, William M. Kelso, Garry Wheeler Stone, and Dell Upton. "Impermanent Architecture in the Southern American Colonies." *Winterthur Portfolio,* XIV (Summer/Autumn, 1981), pp. 135–196.

Carter, Robert, "King." Papers. Manuscripts Division, Special Collections Department, University of Virginia Library, Charlottesville, Va.

Chappell, Edward A. "Social Responsibility and the American History Museum." *Winterthur Portfolio,* XXIV (Winter, 1989), pp. 247–265.

Chippendale, Thomas. *The Gentleman and Cabinetmaker's Director.* Introduction by Ralph Edwards. 3rd ed. London, 1762. Reprint. London: The Connoisseur, 1957.

Cooper, Wendy A. *In Praise of America: American Decorative Arts, 1650–1830.* New York: Alfred A. Knopf, 1980.

Davis, John D. *English Silver at Williamsburg.* Williamsburg, Va.: Colonial Williamsburg Foundation, 1976.

DeNood, Lavinia. "Furnishing Plan for the Nelson House of the Colonial National Historical Park, Yorktown, Virginia." Photocopy of report, 1976.

Dolmetsch, Joan D. *Rebellion and Reconciliation: Satirical Prints on the Revolution at Williamsburg.* Williamsburg, Va.: Colonial Williamsburg Foundation, 1976.

English Conversation Pieces of the Eighteenth Century. Detroit: Detroit Institute of Arts, 1948.

English Pictures for the Country House: An Exhibition of Eighteenth and Early Nineteenth Century Conversation Pieces, Portraits, and Sporting Pictures in Period Rooms . . . London: Leger Galleries, 1986.

Farish, Hunter Dickinson, ed. *The Journal & Letters of Philip Vickers Fithian, 1773–1774: A Plantation Tutor of the Old Dominion.* Williamsburg, Va.: Colonial Williamsburg Foundation, 1957.

Fowler, John, and John Cornforth. *English Decoration in the 18th Century.* London: Barrie & Jenkins Ltd., 1974.

Garrett, Elisabeth Donaghy. *At Home: The American Family, 1750–1870.* New York: Harry N. Abrams, 1990.

Garrett, Elisabeth Donaghy, comp. *The Antiques Book of American Interiors: Colonial and Federal Styles.* New York: Crown Publishers, 1980.

Gilbert, Christopher. *The Life and Work of Thomas Chippendale.* London: Studio Vista in association with Christie, Manson and Woods Ltd., 1978.

Gilbert, Christopher, James Lomax, and Anthony Wells-Cole. *Country House Floors 1660–1850.* Temple Newsam Country House Studies Number 3. Leeds, England: Leeds City Art Galleries, 1987.

Gilbert, Christopher, and Anthony Wells-Cole. *The Fashionable Fireplace, 1660–1840.* Temple Newsam Country House Studies Number 2. Leeds, England: Leeds City Art Galleries, 1985.

Gill, Harold B., Jr., and George M. Curtis III. "Virginia's Colonial Probate Policies and the Preconditions for Economic History." *Virginia Magazine of History and Biography,* LXXXVII (January 1979), pp. 68–73.

Girouard, Mark. *Life in the English Country House: A Social and Architectural History.* New Haven, Conn.: Yale University Press, 1978.

Greene, Jack P., ed. *The Diary of Colonel Landon Carter of Sabine Hall, 1752–1778.* 2 vols. Charlottesville, Va.: University Press of Virginia, 1965.

Greenlaw, Barry A. *New England Furniture at Williamsburg.* Williamsburg, Va.: Colonial Williamsburg Foundation, 1974.

Gusler, Wallace B. *Furniture of Williamsburg and Eastern Virginia, 1710–1790.* Richmond, Va.: Virginia Museum of Fine Arts, 1979.

Harris, Eileen. *Going to Bed.* London: Her Majesty's Stationery Office for the Victoria and Albert Museum, 1981.

_____. *Keeping Warm.* London: Victoria and Albert Museum, 1982.

Hood, Graham. *The Governor's Palace in Williamsburg: A Cultural Study*. Williamsburg, Va.: Colonial Williamsburg Foundation, 1991.

_____. "Refurnishing the Governor's Palace at Colonial Williamsburg." *The Magazine Antiques* (January 1981), pp. 216–223.

_____. "The Role of the British Eighteenth-Century Print at Williamsburg: Introductory Remarks." In *Eighteenth-Century Prints in Colonial America: To Educate and Decorate*. Edited by Joan D. Dolmetsch. Williamsburg, Va.: Colonial Williamsburg Foundation, 1979.

Inventories of Four Eighteenth-Century Houses in the Historic Area of Williamsburg. Williamsburg, Va.: Colonial Williamsburg Foundation, 1974.

Isaac, Rhys. *The Transformation of Virginia, 1740–1790*. Chapel Hill: University of North Carolina Press, 1982.

Jackson-Stops, Gervase. "Johann Zoffany and the Eighteenth-Century Interior." *The Magazine Antiques* (June 1987), pp. 1264–1279.

Lanier, Mildred B. *English and Oriental Carpets at Williamsburg*. Williamsburg, Va.: Colonial Williamsburg Foundation, 1975.

Little, Nina Fletcher. "An Approach to Furnishing." *The Magazine Antiques* (July 1956), pp. 44–46.

Manners & Morals: Hogarth and British Painting 1700–1760. London: Tate Gallery Publications, 1987.

Montgomery, Florence M. "Room Furnishings as Seen in British Prints from the Lewis Walpole Library." Part I: "Bed Hangings"; Part II: "Window Curtains, Upholstery, and Slip Covers." *The Magazine Antiques* (December 1973), pp. 1068–1075; (March 1974), pp. 522–531.

_____. *Textiles in America, 1650–1870*. New York: W. W. Norton, 1984.

Morgan, Edmund S. *Virginians at Home: Family Life in the Eighteenth Century*. Williamsburg, Va.: Colonial Williamsburg Foundation, 1952.

Noël Hume, Ivor. *All the Best Rubbish*. New York: Harper & Row, 1974.

_____. *A Guide to Artifacts of Colonial America*. New York: Alfred E. Knopf, 1978.

_____. *James Geddy and Sons: Colonial Craftsmen*. Williamsburg, Va.: Colonial Williamsburg Foundation, 1970.

_____. *Williamsburg Cabinetmakers: The Archaeological Evidence*. Williamsburg, Va.: Colonial Williamsburg Foundation, 1971.

Paulson, Ronald, comp. *Hogarth's Graphic Works*. 2 vols. New Haven, Conn.: Yale University Press, 1965.

Peirce, Donald C., and Hope Alswang. *American Interiors: New England & the South: Period Rooms at the Brooklyn Museum*. New York: Brooklyn Museum, 1983.

Praz, Mario. *Conversation Pieces: A Survey of the Informal Group Portrait in Europe and America*. London: Methuen & Co Ltd., 1971.

_____. *An Illustrated History of Furnishing from the Renaissance to the 20th Century*. Translated from the Italian by William Weaver. New York: George Braziller, 1964.

_____. *An Illustrated History of Interior Decoration from Pompeii to Art Nouveau*. London: Thames & Hudson, Ltd., 1964.

Quimby, Ian M. G., ed. *Material Culture and the Study of American Life*. New York: W. W. Norton, 1978.

Rice, Kym S. *Early American Taverns: For the Entertainment of Friends and Strangers*. Chicago: Regnery Gateway, 1983.

Riley, Edward Miles, ed. *The Journal of John Harrower: An Indentured Servant in the Colony of Virginia, 1773–1776*. Williamsburg, Va.: Colonial Williamsburg Foundation, 1963.

Roth, Rodris. *Floor Coverings in 18th-Century America*. United States National Museum Bulletin 250. Contributions from the Museum of History and Technology, Paper 59. Washington, D. C.: Smithsonian Press, 1967.

_____. *Tea Drinking in 18th-Century America: Its Etiquette and Equipage*. United States National Museum Bulletin 225. Contributions from the Museum of History and Technology, Paper 14. Washington, D. C.: Smithsonian Press, 1961.

Seale, William. *Recreating the Historic House Interior*. Nashville, Tenn.: American Association for State and Local History, 1979.

Sitwell, Sacheverell. *Conversation Pieces: A Survey of English Domestic Portraits and their Painters*. New York: Charles Scribner's Sons, 1937.

Sorin, Gretchen Sullivan, and Ellen Kirven Donald. *Gadsby's Tavern Museum: Historic Furnishing Plan*. Alexandria, Va.: City of Alexandria, 1980.

Stanard, Mary Newton. *Colonial Virginia: Its People and Customs*. Philadelphia: J. B. Lippincott Company, 1917.

Thornton, Peter. *Authentic Decor: The Domestic Interior 1620–1920*. New York: Viking, 1984.

_____. "Room Arrangements in the Mid-Eighteenth Century." *The Magazine Antiques* (April 1971), pp. 556–561.

_____. *Seventeenth-Century Interior Decoration in England, France, and Holland*. New Haven, Conn.: Yale University Press, 1978.

Upton, Dell. "Vernacular Domestic Architecture in Eighteenth-Century Virginia." *Winterthur Portfolio*, XVII (Summer/Autumn 1982), pp. 95–119.

Walsh, Lorena S. "Urban Amenities and Rural Sufficiency: Living Standards and Consumer Behavior in the Colonial Chesapeake, 1643–1777." *Journal of Economic History*, XLIII (1983), pp. 109–117.

Wenger, Mark R. "The Central Passage in Virginia: Evolution of an Eighteenth-Century Living Space." *In Perspectives in Vernacular Architecture*, II. Edited by Camille Wells. Columbia, Mo.: University of Missouri Press, 1986.

_____. "The Dining Room in Early Virginia." In *Perspectives in Vernacular Architecture*, III. Edited by Thomas Carter and Bernard L. Herman. Columbia, Mo.: University of Missouri Press, 1989.

Whatman, Susanna. *The Housekeeping Book of Susanna Whatman 1776–1800*. Introduction by Christina Hardyment. New ed. London: Century in association with the National Trust, 1987.

Whiffen, Marcus. *The Eighteenth-Century Houses of Williamsburg: A Study of Architecture and Building in the Colonial Capital of Virginia*. Rev. ed. Williamsburg, Va.: Colonial Williamsburg Foundation, 1984.

The Williamsburg Collection of Antique Furnishings. Williamsburg, Va.: Colonial Williamsburg Foundation, 1973.

Woodfin, Maude H., ed. *Another Secret Diary of William Byrd of Westover, 1739–1741: With Letters & Literary Exercises, 1696–1726*. Translated by Marion Tinling. Richmond, Va.: Dietz Press, 1942.

Wright, Louis, and Marion Tinling, eds. *The London Diary (1717–1721) and Other Writings*. New York: Oxford University Press, 1958.

_____. *The Secret Diary of William Byrd of Westover, 1709–1712*. Richmond, Va.: Dietz Press, 1941.

Index

93

61, 78, 79. *See also* Diaries;
  Inventories; Letters; Paintings;
  Prints
Dressers, 76, 77
Dressing glasses, 42, 43, 46
Dressing room, 41, 42
Dressing table. *See* Table, dressing
Dry rubbing, 61; brush, 54, 55, 61
Dundas, Sir Lawrence, 16, 64
Dust, protection against: 12, 14,
  44, 53, 54

Edmonstoun, Col., 53
Eliock, Lord, 53
Elite. *See* Gentry; Upper class
En suite, 56, 59, 81
Everard, Thomas, 18, 49, 80. *See
  also* Brush-Everard House

Fauquier, Lt. Gov. Francis, 12
Field beds, 36
Firebacks, 62
Fireplace tools, 52, 82
Fire screens, 12, 15, 43
Fithian, Philip Vickers, 17, 20, 27,
  29, 47, 48, 53, 81
Floorcloths, 22, 61, 62
Floor plans: of Virginia houses, 10,
  24, 51
Flowers: use of, 60, 63
Forge. *See* Anderson, James
Frederick, Prince (later Duke of
  York), 14, 15
Furniture, 6, 58, 65, 72, 79;
  arrangement of, 5, 7, 11, 12–13,
  15, 18

Gaming, 4. *See also* Cards
Gaol, 2, 3
Gaoler, 2, 3
Gardner, Daniel, 55
Geddy, James, 43, 69, 70
Geddy, James, House, 18, 69, 70,
  71; bedchamber, 43, 44; foundry
  of, 69, 70; shop of, 69, 70
*Gentleman and Cabinet-maker's
  Director, The. See* Chippendale,
  Thomas
Gentry, 23, 25, 49, 50, 51, 67, 73,
  76, 78; life-style of, 4, 8, 74. *See
  also* Upper class
George, Prince of Wales, 14, 15
Glasses. *See* Looking glasses
Glassware, 18, 26, 32
Gordon, Col. James, 82
Governor's Palace: ballroom, 64,
  65; chamber over the dining
  room, 40, 41; closet, 29, 81;
  dining room, 1, 28, 29, 31, 59,

61, 62, 63, 81; His Lordship's
  Bedchamber, 38, 39, 52, 53;
  kitchen, 78; Middle Room
  upstairs, 13, 14, 63; parlor, 62,
  65; refurnishing of, 1; study, 52,
  53, 54, 55; supper room, 64. *See
  also* Berkeley, Norborne, Baron
  de Botetourt; Botetourt
  inventory
Graphics. *See* Documentation
Grates, 12, 48, 62, 63
Guitars, 17, 18
Gunston Hall, 51

Halifax, Lord, 55
Hall, 3, 10, 11, 25, 49, 81
Hamilton, Gawen, 8, 67
Harrower, John, 41
Hay, Anthony, 72, 74, 82;
  cabinetmaking shop of, 72, 73,
  74, 80
Hayward family, 20
Highmore, Joseph, 56, 60
Hogarth, William, 4, 6, 40, 65
Horsehair, 12
Housekeeping manuals, 13, 53, 57,
  61
House of Burgesses, 68
Housewife, 74, 77
Hunter, William, 19
Hussey, Philip, 11

Inns, 46, 47
Inventories, 11, 29, 35, 36, 37, 44,
  47, 57, 61, 79, 81, 82; of
  Bradford, 50; of Hunter, 19; lack
  of, 12, 49; from Northampton
  County, 49; of taverns, 46; use
  of, by curators, 5, 6, 18, 50, 76.
  See also Botetourt inventory;
  Raleigh Tavern; Randolph,
  Peyton, House; Wetherburn's
  Tavern
Irish family, 11

Jefferson, Thomas, 49, 54
Jones, Col. Thomas, 6

Kendall, Joshua, 58
Kidd, Joseph, 62
Kitchen, 74, 76, 77, 78
Kneller, Sir Godfrey, 50

Lath. *See* Pulleys
Laundries, 74, 76
Lee, Francis Lightfoot, 51
Letters, 6, 41
Libraries, 48, 50, 51, 64; of books,
  48, 49, 50, 51, 52, 53, 54, 55.

See also Study
Library of Congress, 54
Light damage, protection from: 14,
  53, 57, 58
Linens, 31, 32, 81. *See also*
  Tablecloths
Lodgings, 46, 47, 81
London, 70, 72, 81
Looking glasses, 12, 19, 23, 26, 28,
  29, 41, 52, 66. *See also*
  Chimney glasses; Dressing
  glasses; Pier glasses; Sconces;
  Swing glasses
Lower class, 8, 25, 30, 69, 74, 76.
  See also Servants; Slaves
Lydia (slave), 74, 82

Map, 52, 53, 54, 55, 65–66; rollers,
  66
Marriage-a-la-Mode, 4, 6
Mattress. *See* Bed
Meals, 3, 27, 28, 30, 31, 32, 49, 74,
  76. *See also* Breakfast; Dessert;
  Dinner; Supper
Menokin, 51
Middling class, 3, 8, 9, 18–19, 44,
  49, 69. *See also* Anderson,
  James; Gaoler; Geddy, James;
  Hay, Anthony; Tradesmen
Mirrors. *See* Looking glasses
Monticello, 54
Mount Airy, 28
Multipurpose use of rooms, 3, 5, 10,
  11, 25, 28, 29, 35, 49
Musical entertainments, 18, 20, 26
Musical instruments, 17. *See also*
  Guitar; Piano

Nails, 65, 71, 72
Nasmyth, Alexander, 53
"Neat and plain," 4
Nelson, Thomas, 62
Nomini Hall, 17, 27
"Noon," 41

Oil cloth. *See* Floorcloths
Outbuildings, 9, 74, 78. *See also*
  Kitchens; Laundries

Paintings, 20, 65; as source, 3, 5, 8,
  15, 64, 79
Pamela, 7, 41, 56, 60
Paper press, 54, 55
Parlor, 23, 24, 29, 35, 55, 80, 81;
  evolution of, 11; furnishings of,
  5, 11, 12, 18–19, 28, 36, 66; use
  of, 4, 11, 17, 19, 25, 28. *See also*
  Brush-Everard House;
  Governor's Palace; Randolph,